Grace Rolls On

Grace Rolls On

a memoir

Paula L. Sturgeon

BEAVER'S POND PRESS

Grace Rolls On © copyright 2012 by Paula L. Sturgeon. All rights reserved. No part of this book may be reproduced in any form whatsoever, by photography or xerography or by any other means, by broadcast or transmission, by translation into any kind of language, nor by recording electronically or otherwise, without permission in writing from the author, except by a reviewer, who may quote brief passages in critical articles or reviews.

Unless otherwise noted, all scripture is from THE HOLY BIBLE, NEW INTERNATIONAL VERSION®, NIV® Copyright © 1973, 1978, 1984, 2011 by Biblical, Inc.™ Used by permission. All rights reserved worldwide.

The Message. Copyright © 1993, 1994, 1995, 1996, 2000, 2001, 2002. Used by permission of NavPress Publishing Group.

New Revised Standard Version Bible, copyright 1989, Division of Christian Education of the National Council of the Churches of Christ in the United States of America. Used by permission. All rights reserved.

"I Was There to Hear Your Borning Cry," John Ylvisaker. Used by permission.

"Dancing Queen" Copyright: Lyrics © Universal Music Publishing Group, EMI Music Publishing. Songwriters: ANDERSSON, BENNY GORAN BROR/ULVAEUS, BJOERN K./ANDERSON, STIG/NEBOT, NICOLAS

"You Light Up My Life" Copyright: Lyrics © Warner/Chappell Music, Inc., MIKE CURB MUSIC, Universal Music Publishing Group. Songwriter: BROOKS, JOE

"Que Sera Sera" Copyright: Lyrics © Warner/Chappell Music, Inc. Songwriters: LIVINGSTON, JAY/EVANS, RAY

ISBN: 978-1-59298-499-2
Library of Congress Control Number: 2012908157

Book design by Ryan Scheife, Mayfly Design
Typeset in Bembo
Printed in the United States of America
First Printing: 2012

16   15   14   13   12   5   4   3   2   1

Beaver's Pond Press, Inc.
7108 Ohms Lane
Edina, MN 55439-2129
(952) 829-8818
www.BeaversPondPress.com

To order, visit www.BeaversPondBooks.com
or call (800) 901-3480. Reseller discounts available.

www.GraceRollsOn.com

For my mother,
You were there in the beginning,
and have been there through all the lows and all the highs.
We share this story
and I thank God for you.

With all my love.

Contents

Preface ix

1. Picture Perfect 1
2. The Promise from My Mother 11
3. Babies and a Bouffant 21
4. Growing Up Gimpy 31
5. The Parts in-Between 61
6. What I Found in Texas 73
7. How I Learned to be a Lutheran 89
8. Hello Paula, God Calling…A Big Story in Three Parts 103
9. Becoming Miss Paula 137
10. Go With the Flow 151
11. "Just a Bunch of Church Hags" 171
12. Hey, Now I'm a Rock Star 185
13. When Gimpy Gets Gloomy 213
14. A Fool and Her Leg are Soon Parted 223
15. The Promise from My Father 255
16. When Losing the Battle Means Winning the War 267

Postscript 289
A Letter to My Grandmother 294
About the Author 297

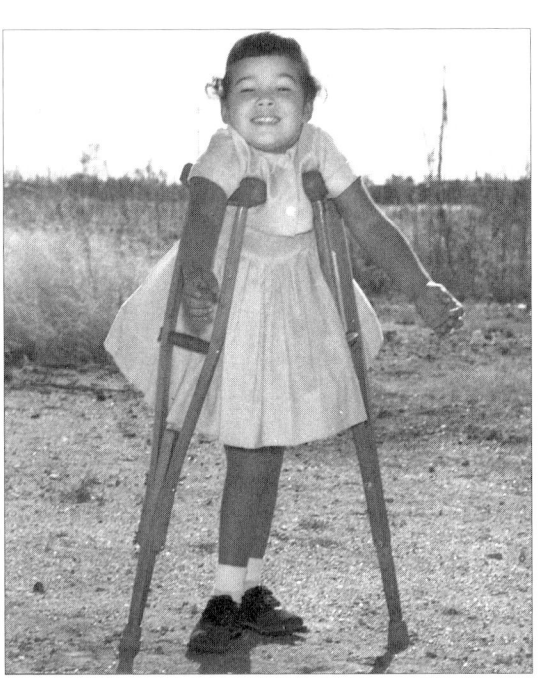

Preface

Before you read any further...

My sense of humor is my stock in trade. I love to laugh, and do so whenever possible. The ability to laugh comes from my somewhat cockeyed worldview. This allows me to find humor in some of the most unlikely places. I have no patience for the "politically correct" viewpoint. Everything has a comic perspective, if we but choose to see it. Certainly, not all of life is funny. Yet I survive the toughest times through a willingness to laugh. As you read this book, I hope you are able to find humor in some of those same odd places. Feel free to laugh! But, if doing so makes you feel uncomfortable or even a bit guilty, blame it on me. I can take it.

There may also be tears. I hope there are portions of this story that move you. Life comes with tears and I, for one, refuse to run from those situations.

Also—hard as I tried—I could not avoid my tendency to write the way I speak. Public speaking is what I do. Writing is not. I have written this book as though I were having a conversation. I have worked hard to be authentic. Less of my energy has been placed on sentence structure. My editors have done wonderful work fixing some of my fragments, yet I am certain there remain some choppy spots. For some, that may be painful. Please accept my apologies.

So, my friend, if you dare, turn the page and share this conversation with me.

I

Picture Perfect

Most of all, love each other as if your life depended on it. Love makes up for practically anything.

—1 Peter 4:8 (The Message)

Perfect—picture perfect—for many of my generation (baby boomers), this is how we might describe the 1950s. We do so, for the most part, without benefit of real firsthand experience. Although I was born in the fifties (1956 to be exact) I have no real memories of my own life in those days—and, certainly, no firsthand knowledge of that decade.

My knowledge of the fifties comes primarily from televised shows like *Leave It to Beaver* and later, *Happy Days*. The formula for those shows was drawn directly from the reality occurring in mid-America at the time. Dad worked, mom stayed home, and children played blissfully inside white picket fences. It seemed so simple.

Of course there was far more going on in the world. The Cold War and the spread of Communism were leading both the national and international headlines. War on the Korean Peninsula ended and conflict soon became war in Vietnam. Children's play was too often overshadowed by the great plague of the times—polio.

Into this world of seeming contradiction, I was born. The firstborn child of Paul and Mary Lee Sturgeon, my birth was not exactly planned. My parents were not Ward and June Cleaver. We did not have a picket fence.

My father was a salesman and my mother worked for the government. They lived in an apartment in the upstairs of my grandmother's house. They, like most young couples, struggled financially, and a baby didn't fit into the budget. Mama was ready for motherhood. I think she was born ready. My dad was not at all ready. It took almost thirty years for him to appreciate and enjoy fatherhood.

This is the backdrop for a very cold night in January. My father and grandmother took my mother to the hospital to give birth to me. The story is that my dad was a nervous wreck and that Mama did all the work.

Before I was born, there had been disagreement between them about my name. Mama wanted to name me Sarah. Daddy didn't like that and preferred to call me Laura. I'm told there wasn't much argument between them. Rather, Mama simply announced to my father that she had named the baby.

Now, my mother has a certain tone of voice that, when used to make such announcements or decrees, indicates that debate is futile. Such was the case as she told my father I was to be named Paula. She did so in the hope that he would remain clear about his responsibility. I was not just his daughter, nor simply his firstborn child; I was now his namesake. He understood, accepted the decision, and didn't argue. Smart guy!

At the end of her weeklong stay in the hospital (the standard for those days) my father came to take us home.

The nurse preparing for our discharge took me from the bassinet and placed me in my father's arms. With a strong German accent, she pronounced that "Da papa vil take home da baby." Later in his life, my father said that this was the moment he realized how much his life had changed.

Now named and at home, I was loved fully and completely by Mama and Daddy. My great grandmother also lived with my grandmother, and I had aunts and uncles and Mama's large extended family to love me.

Mama quit working and became a stay-at-home mom, and we began a lifelong journey together. The nature of our relationship extends beyond the kind of traditional definitions that are all too often limiting. You could say she is more than just my mother; she is also my nurse, cattle prod, companion, confessor, and more. And you would be correct in all of those instances. In a later chapter, I share more about this magnificent woman and her role in my life.

"Baby talk" didn't happen in our home. My parents (including my grandmother) spoke to me in the King's English. With full sentences and proper grammar, they spoke to me in the same manner they would speak to others. Daddy read Shakespeare to me more frequently than children's books. I knew Portia's soliloquy on the quality of mercy from *The Merchant of Venice* long before I was required to recite it from memory for a college Shakespeare class. He loved poetry and regularly quoted from memory some of the passages he loved. Daddy had a wonderful voice, which he could and would modulate in order to achieve dramatic results. As a child,

I remember hearing, "Send not to know for whom the bell tolls, it tolls for thee." I had no idea what John Donne's words meant, or the power behind them, but they were beautiful to hear from my father's lips.

It should come as no surprise that I began to speak at an early age. As an only child and surrounded by adults, I spoke in complete sentences practically from the start. Albeit with a small vocabulary, I was able to communicate. No brag, just fact.

And the bragging—I mean fact sharing—continues: I never crawled; I walked on my own when I was ten months old. I hit all the developmental markers significantly ahead of schedule. My early physical achievements seem almost tragic when compared to my current physical circumstance.

One more —if you can stand it: I was potty trained by my first birthday. Mama sat me on the training potty whenever she went to the bathroom at home. The story goes that one day she took me to visit my grandmother who was an associate buyer in the children's section of a local department store. While Mama and Grandmother chatted, I wandered off. Finding a little pink training potty, I sat down and did my business. I knew what a potty was for, although I didn't fully grasp the need to remove some clothing. When Mama and Grandmother found me, I was sitting (proudly) in wet clothes. Mama decided that was a clear sign that I was ready for full potty training.

One year old and I was walking, talking, and potty trained. Loved and adorable. It was picture perfect. Until…

At fourteen months of age, I was diagnosed with polio. Polio—the word struck fear and panic in the hearts of parents in those days. It could be devastating and even deadly. I'd had two of the three vaccine doses, which made the diagnosis all the more shocking. Following a bout with fever and general illness, I showed atrophy in my left leg. Retrospectively, the doctors felt certain that it was indeed polio. But, it was such a minor case, with minimal muscle atrophy in the left calf. There was now cause for elation where there could have been despair.

Joy can be all too short lived. Joy bubbles into the scenario of our lives, bringing with it hope and possibility. When the joy bubble bursts (as it inevitably does), we are easily surprised when difficulty steps into its place. So it was for my family when, two months later, I began to experience pain in my right leg. Mama said I didn't actually complain about pain; rather, I walked with my leg bent and used my tiptoes to stand. Perhaps I didn't want to walk properly because it hurt. The once-active child was now slowed. One evening my grandmother also noticed that my knee was "hot" to the touch. My symptoms were worse in the morning and eased as the day went on, only to return the next morning. What could be happening?

So it was back to the doctor. Physical examination and blood tests revealed that I had Still's disease. This was the term at the time for rheumatoid arthritis in children.

Upon hearing the diagnosis, my mother breathed a sigh of relief. She had feared the worst, cancer or perhaps tuberculosis of the bone. She had feared that I would die. Thanks be to God, this would not kill me.

Ironically, I believe it is my mother's attitude that has framed and informed my entire life. Bad as the diagnosis was, it would not kill me.

Diagnosis made. The race to find what was best for me now began. My mother wrote a letter to Dr. Still in England to ask his guidance. He wrote back that he, regretfully, had nothing to offer. He believed that in time, research might one day yield an answer.

My parents began to search for something, anything they could do for me. Out of that search came the idea of moving to a warmer climate. The question of moving from Kansas to Arizona was debated with physicians on both sides of the argument. Our family doctor told my parents, "The road to the desert is littered with the bones of people who went there to be cured." The orthopedic surgeon's response was quite different. He said that if I were his child, he would move to the West because "there are physicians there who will see and treat many more cases like this than I shall ever see in my practice." That argument won the day.

Family dynamics now shifted into high gear. My father sought a transfer from Kansas City, Kansas, to Tucson, Arizona. Mama's sister Carol, suffering from asthma, decided to move as well. Carol's husband (Uncle Dallas) worked for the railroad and was able to procure passes for Mama and me and Carol, and her seven-month-old daughter (my cousin), Amy. The women moved immediately and the men followed as soon as transfers allowed.

On December 1, 1957, we arrived in Tucson, Arizona. We had left the cold of Kansas and arrived to see ornamental orange trees. "Mama, see the Merry Christmas trees," was my first comment. *(Cute, huh?)*

People with whom my father would eventually work at Mutual of Omaha met us. Gracious and kind, they helped Mama and Aunt Carol find a place to live, shop, and even worship. They also suggested a pediatrician.

I look back on that time with tremendous admiration

for my mother and my aunt. How courageous it was to leave their husbands and extended family, and the place where they grew up. They moved from a place of seasons, green grass, trees, and, most of all, familiarity to a world where everything was different.

These amazing women were taking charge of their lives and families. Despite limited financial resources, they were determined to make life good for us. They faced each day with their strongest tools: faith and love.

Our family was blessed with two families in Tucson whose support was invaluable. One family was my father's boss and his wife. The other was the boss' friend's family, including a son, a few years older than I, who had been diagnosed with arthritis. Through these wonderful people, we met my physicians.

My pediatrician was Hugh Thompson. He was tall with a booming voice, which could instantly become soft and gentle when dealing with a child. Mother says he could scare parents and calm children in equal measure. John Schwartzmann, a former collegiate football player with a loud, deep voice and a brusque personality, became my orthopedic surgeon. Despite his outward appearance to the contrary, he treated me with gentleness and kindness. The third member of the care team was Donald Hill, a rheumatologist. After about a year, he admitted that he had (in his own words) "gone soft" and turned my care over to his partner, Robert Johnson. Both Hill and Johnson were tender and compassionate men.

It's hard enough to get two doctors to agree—imagine how tough it was for three. Particularly these three men, and these three medical/surgical specialties.

By the grace of God they did, and set about a plan of care that would enable me to live an active life and protect my joints from the ravages of the disease. This was no easy task. Each had a role to play, and each deserve a portion of the credit for the life I've been able to live.

A key component of this plan was surgical intervention to save and stabilize my joints. It took great courage for my mother and father to say yes to surgery. In so doing, surgeons hoped to save my joints for the technical advances that would come along twenty-five years later. Dr. Schwartzmann began with straightening the right leg and fusing the bones together. It meant my knee wouldn't bend, but it would be straight and strong. And most importantly, I could walk on it with significantly less pain. Shortly thereafter, both ankles were fused for the same reason. There would be surgeries to realign bones and joints. Casts, crutches, and a wheelchair were my constant companions.

Drs. Thompson and Johnson managed the medical side of the program. They tried gold salts, cortisone shots, and good old aspirin therapy. I learned to swallow a pill at a very young age. Some worked better than others.

I grew up in and around the hospital and could write a firsthand account of the evolution of the bedpan. Between doctors and therapists, I wish I had a dollar for every hour I spent as a healthcare consumer. By my fifth birthday, the pattern for my life was set. There would always be doctors' appointments and medications. Surgery would be required to hold off the changes in my body from the disease and to respond to the changes resulting simply from growth.

Pain would also be a constant factor in my life. Some days would be good with little limitations and others would be fiercely challenging. Sometimes the medications worked, other times not. No two days were the same. That uncertainty challenged me more as I grew older. Children roll with it better than adults, I suppose. Adults, however, have jobs and commitments, which generally require some consistency. The disease of rheumatoid arthritis is facile, ever-changing. The only constant: uncertainty of what the next day will hold.

So that's how it began. From picture-perfect to something far from perfect. The facts of my story are pretty straightforward. Disease comes to many, and in some way touches all of our lives. That's the way life goes. This is the human condition.

Perhaps you are asking this question: how did a toddler with the devastating diagnosis of juvenile rheumatoid arthritis become a happy, successful woman?

The answer is: it's not about the disease. Like my mother, who was relieved by my diagnosis (at least it would not kill me), perspective is critical. The disease is a *part* of my story. It is not, however, *the* story.

Think and reflect for a moment about this: what is "*the* thing" that is the key ingredient in your life? Don't look to the obvious (like my disease); rather, consider the totality of your life. Reflect on what is "*the* thing" that, if missing, would have drastically changed your life path. Then, you will have the key ingredient.

From my first breath, the essential ingredient in my life has been love. Generous, gracious, freewheeling love. In all my life, my strongest sense has been a feeling of being loved.

And not just any love—God's love.

Good and gracious God,
Creator of life,

I give you thanks and praise
for the way in which You have kneaded me together.
Let Your Holy Spirit abide.
Enable me to see the big picture of my life
and lead me to an attitude of thanks and praise.
In Your love I dwell.

Amen

2

The Promise from My Mother

Whatever will be, will be
The future's not ours, to see

—from a song my mother sang to me as a child

There comes a time in the life of all children (and especially a crippled child) when questions of a serious nature will be asked and must be answered. Not the simple "there there" or "it will be okay" answers for which children and even adults all too often settle. Serious questions arise out of serious concern and experience. Having lived in the midst of it all, I believe one earns the right to ask for serious answers. Eventually a critical question may surface, the answer for which may be life changing. All children have them and deserve a person in their life to whom they may turn, and from whom they receive the critical answer.

From the very earliest days of my illness, my mother laid the groundwork for such questioning. She told doctors, nurses, and technicians that they must explain what they were about to do before they began. This didn't always go over well. Medical professionals generally preferred quiet, compliant patients. Children should be seen and not heard was not simply social etiquette; it was (and remains) the prevailing expectation in medicine. Mama's voice could calm and soothe me in those moments of anxiety, which are common for children in the midst of the healthcare machine. You are small and defenseless. People around you, who are charged with helping you feel better, often hurt you. This is the all-too-harsh reality. Anxiety begins in direct proportion to the extent of the uncertainty being faced.

Beyond anxiety, there were also moments of pure abject terror. Fear takes anxiety and adds the element of helplessness. Anxiety is wondering if it will hurt. Fear is remembering the last time, how it hurt, and not knowing how long the pain will last this time. When that sort of fear took over, Mama could and would gently yet firmly set me back into place. She was (and is) a pragmatic realist. In this regard particularly, she is much like her mother. Without any harsh attitude and in a very calm, matter-of-fact manner, she would say, "If this is what it takes to get better, then this is what we are going to do."

There were times when Mama was a cheerleader without pom poms. When the surgeon suggested yet another operation, Mama kicked into the full "YIPPEE" mode. The ride home was filled with her chatter of how exciting this was, and how wonderful things would be as a result. It was almost impossible to not trust her. She seemed so certain.

Early on, I learned about needles. Before the advent of disposables, needles were sterilized and reused. Older needles developed microscopic burrs, and thus were more painful. I knew always to ask for new needles before blood draws and IVs. When they were unavailable, I asked the technician to show me that the needle was all right by drawing the needle across a piece of cotton. If the needle didn't snag the cotton, it was good, meaning no painful burrs.

On those occasions when a medical professional refused (sometimes belligerently) to play by my "advised consent," there were vocal protestations on my part. Generally, this was done with the support of my parents. Mama had told them to explain first and, if they didn't listen to her, she didn't mind them getting an earful from me. On those occasions, my advanced verbal skills were of great value. Perhaps that was just true for me and not so much for the poor technician, nurse, or even physician who wasn't in the mood for my verbal diatribes.

Standing up for myself was something that both Mama and Daddy encouraged. And so was respect. Respect was demanded more than encouraged. I was raised to say "Yes sir" and "No ma'am." Please and thank you were not just "magic words," they were an expectation. Adults were to be shown respect, and that began with speaking to them in a proper fashion. My father was raised in the South and Mama in the Midwest. It is no small wonder, therefore, that manners were standard operating principles.

Mama and I had occasion to spend lots of time together. From doctors' offices to laboratories, we spent significant time in waiting rooms. These rooms are aptly named. Waiting is something you do plenty of when you are a healthcare consumer. That's just a reality.

By the way, I am generally a good "waiter." I know that doctors are not sitting around thinking of ways to slow down. Any patient who takes extra time with their physician, and then complains about waiting, gets no sympathy from me. So, the next time you are waiting, try relaxing, breathing, and perhaps say a prayer of gratitude for living where you can get great healthcare. But I digress; back to the story.

Mama was my pal, my buddy, and pretty much my constant companion. To that relationship, add my clear understanding that she was also my mother. From those bonds was forged the kind of trust that is all too often late in coming to parents and children. This was more than childlike devotion to a loving parent. Early on, I somehow knew that my mom was the person on whom I could always rely.

My father was a loving parent, and I was a "Daddy's girl." He treated me like a princess and so long as I was respectful, with good manners, my daddy was pleased with me. He would gladly have taken my pain, and he did everything he could to show me great love.

So how was this different from my mother? She too would have taken my pain and loved me mightily. On the surface, the only noticeable difference between my mama and my daddy was the amount of time we spent together. Daddy went to work, Mama stayed at home. Remember, this was the 1950s.

As an adult, this is what I know of the difference in my relationships with my mama and daddy. He wanted the arthritis to go away, and lived in the hope that each surgery or new drug would be the magic cure. Mama, on the other hand, prayed for cures while diligently striving for ways to help me live with the disease. And not only live with the disease, but live a normal life.

Daddy treated me as special. Mama treated me as normal.

I was a "chatty" child. I liked to be in conversation. Talk—talk—talk—that was me. Truth be told, it still is. And, when nervous or upset, both then and now, I become extremely verbal. *(Those who know me personally are cordially invited to stop laughing.)*

I would also talk to just about anybody. Perhaps an early indication of my extroversion was my desire to strike up a conversation with anyone. My love of talking was exceeded only by my love of being the center of attention. Cute and chatty, these are the attributes that make a grandparent proud.

My poor mother was my primary conversation partner. We could and would talk about anything and everything. Of course, there were times when my health dominated our discourse. From aches and pains to figuring out ways to get my socks on, there were so many things we shared.

My health was not, by any measure, our principal topic. Mama talked with me about all sorts of things. Current events were important in our lives. *The Huntley-Brinkley Report* was appointment television.

I loved stories of family and times past. Both my father and my grandmother were great storytellers. Generally, a good storyteller needs very little encouragement to begin, but they both loved when I asked to have the same story told over and over again. Stories of my father's life of economic poverty were rich with great characters. They helped me to understand where I came from, and build gratitude for what we had. When Grandmother and Mama spoke about my grandfather, I felt connected to the man they loved and I never met.

Around the kitchen table we talked about everything. No question and no topic were out of bounds. And because we talked about everything, I knew I could ask anything. I had faith that I would get a truthful answer.

My critical-question moment came when I was five years old. There was no particular trigger or situation that prompted this question. My mother recalls that it seemed to come out of nowhere. There was no way she could have anticipated my question, and consequently had no ready, pre-packed answer. Every child asks where babies come from, so most parents are ready with an answer, such as "The twinkle in your father's eye." Generally speaking, the question isn't nearly as important as the answer. A good answer (to any question) does more than convey facts; it serves to further a sense of settlement and peace. It is the "stuff" upon which relationships are built.

This was my critical question: "Mama, when is the arthritis going to go away?"

WOW! What a question. As I write this today, I can only imagine the "gut check" that must have happened for my mother. Yes, she knew the factual answer, but who would want to have that conversation with a child?

If you are a parent, hope to be a parent, or have ever loved a child, imagine for a moment having such a difficult conversation. Knowing that your answer could be heartbreaking and perhaps even life altering is onerous. I can only thank the Lord for my mama, yet again.

"When is the arthritis going away?" Such an innocent question. Such a cruel answer. Who would want to tell a child such bad news? This was my mother's dilemma. How could she tell this child she loved that her life would always be impacted by this disease? Mother had worked in and around medicine, and knew the prognosis was bleak. Doctors had told her there was no cure, and furthermore no way to predict future disease progression and consequent joint destruction. Any other questions seem preferable to this one.

And yet in these moments, Christ is present. From John 1:5: *The light shines in the darkness, and the darkness has not overcome it.*

The light shone and the answer was given to mother to give to me. Guided by God's Holy Spirit and supported by the Saints in light, she began, "Well, honey, it isn't going to go away. Arthritis is a sickness your body is going to have for your whole life."

"But," she continued, "this is what I want you to remember—most especially: God will always be with you and watch over you. He will help you when it is hard. And I make you this promise: as long as He sees fit, I will be with you also, and together with God you will be all right."

Five-year-olds have a marvelous capacity to accept such direct and love-filled answers. Candy is good. Candy coating the truth is not. My response was simple acceptance. Mama tells me that I replied "okay" and went back to whatever activity (neither of us remember exactly) I was doing. Question asked and answered. It was just that simple.

I cry every time I retell this story. I marvel at the grace and courage it took to be so honest. And I give thanks for her witness and truth telling.

Mama's promise to me so many years ago set the stage for all that would come in my life. Certainly, she gave me clarity. But more than that, she gave me a very special strength, the strength that comes from knowing I would never really be alone. Someone would always have my back. Between the good Lord and my mother, there wasn't anything that could destroy me. Mama and the

Lord—talk about a dynamic duo! I was on solid footing.

Times would come when loneliness hit me. As I examine those times through the lens of retrospection, I'm startled at what I see. Loneliness often came when my faith life was in an "inactive mode." Knowing and appreciating God's abiding presence is crucial to my life. A relationship with a loving God, as revealed to me through Jesus, means I am never alone.

Today I make my home with my mother. She has always been a steady presence in my life and has been there for me through it all. Sometimes she cheers me on. Other times she encourages me with a well-deserved kick in the pants. She has always kept her promise.

And so has God. His unfailing love has been the truth of my life. Through all of life's turns and twists, the Lord has brought me the peace of mind to keep on keeping on. He has placed amazing people and wonderful experiences in my journey; for this and more, I give thanks and praise.

May I ask a critical question? Are you afraid of the dark? I don't mean the part of the day when Mr. Sun has gone to bed. I mean the dark places of your life, and perhaps even those inside your heart. They may be events and/or circumstances that provoke feelings of despair and sadness. Sometimes we may even feel victimized by them.

What if we were to examine the darkness as the absence of light, that place where you have feelings of being alone and without a way into the future? This may be a perceived lack of something, which (like glue) holds you in your darkness. Or you may think there is something dark that has the power to hold you down and keep you from reaching out to touch the light.

Let's consider stepping outside of the darkness in the perspective of our faith. Jesus is the light of the world. It is through His life that we may fully understand real darkness. He was nailed to a cross, died the most excruciatingly painful death, and was then buried in a stone-closed tomb. Yet neither the cross nor the tomb could contain the light. Jesus' triumph over darkness and death enables each of us to seek the light in our own lives. This is the truth around which our faith is formed.

As a child, I was far less theologically oriented than I am now. It was the simple faith of my mother as she shared it with me that enabled me to face the darkness. Do not forget the power of asking the hard critical questions which, when answered, may be just the light needed to bring you forward.

Sometimes the question must be asked of others. Then there are those that must be asked and answered only by you. Take that step and know *the* light is always on.

*Good and gracious God,
Almighty Lord,*

*You are the source and giver of light and truth,
and yet we confess, Lord, that we too readily
fear the light and hide in the dark.
In all our circumstances may we recognize
Your presence and power
to move us and change us
to calm us and cheer us
to lead us out of the darkness and into your light.*

*And as always, Father, I give You thanks for my mother.
You know, Lord, You know.*

Amen

3

Babies and a Bouffant

I was there to hear your borning cry,
I'll be there when you are old.
I rejoiced the day you were baptized,
to see your life unfold.

"I Was There to Hear Your Borning Cry"

by John Ylvisaker

Embarrassed—humiliated—mortified. You pick the word because any and all of them could easily be used to describe the way I felt that Maundy Thursday evening as I waited to be baptized. My parents were putting me through this miserable experience, and I was not a happy preteen. Did I hate the idea of getting baptized? Well—noooo—duh! Oh my gosh, I am regressing to some sort of ancient teen-speak just thinking about that night.

Of course I knew being baptized was important. I had completed communicant studies and had been endorsed by the lay leaders of our Presbyterian congregation, the Session. So what was the big deal? I was to be baptized with babies. Babies—cute, adorable babies. Babies—wearing long white baptismal gowns and caps (no doubt family heirlooms) and wrapped in beautiful blankets and lovingly cradled in their parents' arms. They were, quite simply, gorgeous, perfect babies.

The "oohs and aahs" fluttered in the air as these babies were brought forward to the baptismal font. I should have known that all eyes would be fixed on little Michael and little Kathy. They were, after all, the joys of so many people. What a great night this would be! God's promises were coming to these precious children, truly an act of amazing grace for His most innocent. It was all so wonderful—for those families and their babies. Not so for me. Why? I WAS NOT A BABY!

I was twelve years old—almost a teenager—and clearly not that far from being an adult. Certainly I did not belong in a group of babies.

Rather than an heirloom baptismal gown, I was wearing a sailor dress. It was navy blue with white polka dots, wide collar, and drop neck sash. You may remember the sixties. UGH! My mother chose it and persuaded me to wear it by promising me new shoes. Now, that sounds great, but you must know that the shoe-buying experience is traumatic in and of itself. The great challenge in the process is my deformed (and by that I mean flat, size six EEEE) feet. I often deflect the emotional trauma of shoe shopping by asking the sales associate to simply "lace up the boxes." It is a joke. Like all good humor, however, it belies a real truth. My feet are short, flat, and fat.

With Mother's can-do attitude, we managed to find a pair of white patent-leather (one-inch heel) pumps with a grosgrain ribbon bow on the toe. Raise your hand if you've ever had a pair of these shoes. Hang your head if you still have a pair in your closet.

CAUTION: Reading further requires a strong constitution. Conjure this image only if you dare. There I stood in my sailor dress and killer shoes (one inch seems almost flat to most, but to me it was a painfully high heel), and the look was completed with a sort of cherry on top: I had a bouffant hairdo that was easily three-feet high. Well, maybe not, but suffice it to say it was big. I was aware of this fact as I looked around at the babies. My hair was as big as many of them. My big body with my black hair done up in a big bouffant made it hard to hide in the background. And, have I said enough that my dress was dorky and my feet were killing me? Okay—maybe I have.

The babies and I were about to be the center of attention. We were about to be brought into the family of God through the sacrament of Holy Baptism. As I write this, I am keenly aware of the importance of that day. And I am more than a little sad—sad that I had not been one of those babies. Sad too for what my parents went through to get to this day.

This public moment came about as a result of a private moment between my mom and dad. Following an ill-fated meeting between my parents and the pastor of a previous congregation, it is remarkable that I was even being baptized. My parents met with the senior pastor of that previous congregation to discuss membership for my parents and my baptism. After the preliminary pleasantries, my father characteristically got straight to his point. He asked the pastor, "Explain how God would allow something like this (referring to my arthritis) to happen to a child."

With what is most certainly a dreadful misinterpretation, the pastor replied, "Oh father, scripture is most clear on this. The sins of the fathers are visited on the children. The question must therefore be asked of ourselves rather than of God."

My father's succinct response was, "The God I worship would not punish a child for something I have done." *(Right on, Daddy!)*

A miracle occurred that day: my father left without punching the pastor. Daddy was not willing to have me baptized. Not by that pastor and not at that church.

My father did not exactly go into that meeting with happy feelings about the church. In full disclosure, many of my father's feelings were also a result of a kaleidoscope of childhood issues, which all too often grow from a kind of petri dish. By this I mean the kind of medium wherein faith, church, and relationships with and between mother and father are mixed. My paternal grandmother was a devout Christian woman who raised her children in a conservative Baptist church. My paternal grandfather, as the story goes, was drawn to and became involved in the evangelistic movement and regularly preached at tent revivals. It is no small wonder, as I look back, that my father was neither able to speak of his faith nor teach it to his children. The only thing from his youth that he could say, no doubt influenced by his sainted mother, was that baptism ought to be a choice made by the baptized based upon their own understanding of faith. Daddy did not want me baptized as a baby. His attitude toward faith, which ranged from animosity to ambiguity, did not change appreciably until the later days of his life.

My mother had wanted me to be one of those adorable pink bundles. She wanted that public celebration of God's blessings. Her own commitment to God began early in her life and was nurtured along the way by both her family and a supportive church family. Mama's faith was and is deeply personal, and something she wished for her children.

I remember how she smiled when she told stories of her life in the church. There was the zany pastor whose driving both frightened and delighted his passengers— and the honor she felt on attending a Christian Endeavor meeting with the thrill of staying in college dorm rooms. She sang songs to me from those days and quoted scripture she had memorized as a child from the King James Version.

Growing up without a father (Mama's father died when she was eleven) meant that two important needs had to be met by the church. First, my mother and her brother and sister were assured that a loving God would watch over them. In preaching and in teaching, in small and large ways, they heard the words of Jesus, from John 14:18: *I will not leave you as orphans; I will come to you.*

Secondly, the church provided a sort of extended family around this little nuclear family. The men and women of the church needed to step in and support (as prescribed in scripture) the widow and her children. God, in His infinite wisdom, plans for things we are incapable of imagining.

My mother wanted me to have the support of that kind of Christian community. The problem was,—when my father said no, he meant it. Debate was futile. (This fact I grew to understand all the more as a teenager.) My father would not be moved. My mother was and is essentially a pragmatist, and therefore resigned herself to the reality that there would be no public baptism of her baby. Mary Lee also subscribes to the great American philosophy of "Where there is a WILL there is a WAY."

It was that WILL that came through on one particular afternoon. I was about two years old. With tears in her eyes and a heartfelt understanding of the gravity of what she was about to do, she took me into the bathroom. Then, while running water into the sink, she held me close and began speaking to God. The words she prayed that day are cherished treasures to me. *Dear Lord, you gave me the gift of this child and I thank you so. Now I want you to know that, with love, I give her back to you.*

Then, while pouring water on my head, she continued saying, "I baptize you in the name of God, Father, Son, and Holy Spirit. Amen."

In that moment and in her heart, I was given to God, and all of His promises were given to me. I became a baptized child of God.

The late President Ronald Reagan was famous for saying, "In God we trust, all others must document." As I neared the end of the Communicant Training class and would soon be able to participate in the Lord's Supper, the question came from the pastor (different pastor and congregation from the earlier unpleasantness) to my parents. When and where was she baptized? I knew I had no baptismal papers. How would they answer that question? Would it mean that I had wasted time learning all that stuff for nothing?

Re-enter pragmatic Mary Lee. Is lying to the pastor the same as lying to God? Mama went through her decision tree in lightning speed. She swallowed hard and said, "She hasn't been." What else could she say? This was neither the time to tell my father what she had done, nor was it the time to discuss or argue the theological underpinnings of baptism with the pastor.

"Okay, then," Pastor said. "We will get her baptized on Maundy Thursday with the other children." Who was he kidding? I was a child, and the "others" were babies.

So it was. There I stood on Maundy Thursday, front and center, in my sailor dress, killer shoes, and bouffant hairdo, amid all those babies.

Despite my discomfort, I recall feeling that something special was happening. Certainly, I could not articulate the theological importance of the moment. This awareness didn't come from "acing" Baptism 101. It was years before I could fully appreciate all that went into my journey to that particular Maundy Thursday evening.

I realized something special was happening when I stopped looking at my own discomfort and started looking around the room at the faces of the people in the congregation. The moms and the dads, grandparents, and other loved ones of those to be baptized had shiny moist eyes. And, they were not alone. Most of the congregation seemed to radiate warmth. There were grins and nods everywhere I looked. Their faces spoke silent soliloquies of love. We love you. God loves you. You are special. Somehow I just knew that was what they were thinking.

Then I saw my own family. Daddy was calm and my grandmother had her usual "Queen Mum" smile. Mama had tears in her eyes. Her tears were not of sorrow but rather came from that place of pure joy and elation. This public moment meant the realization of a long-held desire. Her wish was for me to have the full experience of Christian community. In the same way she had as a preteen, she knew the support of a faith family would be critical for me. If not that day—then one day. As my life continues to unfold for me, the importance of that day and my gratitude for that moment grows.

I tell this story in my speeches and, in the question-and-answer session following, I am almost always asked, which baptism counted? Was it the one performed by my mother in the bathroom sink—or —the one performed by the ordained clergyman in a church at a baptismal font? Knowing that the question is coming enables me to keep an important scripture reference at the ready. From Ephesians 4:4–6: *There is one body and one Spirit, just as you were called to one hope when you were called, one Lord, one faith, one baptism, one God and Father of all, who over all and through all and in all.* In our Lutheran worship, we confess, from the Nicene Creed: "We acknowledge one baptism for the remission of sins…"

If we accept, as Martin Luther wrote in the Small Catechism, that baptism occurs when water and the Word of God come together. Well then…

*Good and gracious God,
Lord of all life,*

*Allow me the grace to walk in the beauty of Your love.
Take those moments which seem less than ideal
and give me vision to see them in their full potential.
For the treasure which is found in You,
through the Water and the Word
allow Your promise to be real in my life.
Empower me to walk forever with You.*

Amen

4

Growing Up Gimpy

For you created my inmost being;
you knit me together in my mother's womb.
I praise you because I am fearfully and wonderfully made;
your works are wonderful,
I know that full well…

—Psalm 139:13-14a

Nicknames. Love them or hate them, we all get them at some point in our lives. They can be given with affection or come from the cutting edge of a sharp tongue. And, all too often, a nickname outlives its welcome. My nickname was Sweet Pea, and eventually it was shortened to Pete. My mom called me Petey, as did Aunt Carol. For the most part, cousins and others in the family stuck with Pete. It never caught on outside of the family. It even, with a few exceptions, faded within the family. When I hear "Petey," I smile. It was and is a good nickname.

My mother had one other nickname for me that she used with affection. I was her "little cripple" or "little gimp." Mama knew all too well that words like "cripple" and "gimp" were words I was going to hear from others. She hoped that having heard them first from her, the sting from others would be lessened. Mama knew that our all-too-cruel world would have tough words for a child with "differences." She also felt I could be strong enough to handle them. "Cripple" and "gimp" are words that make some people squeamish. They feel harsh and unkind. I understand that. And yet, I also hope people will understand that these are merely words. Further, they are now words of *my* choosing. I embrace them. I am generally uncomfortable with the terms that society has from time to time embraced to describe people with physical challenges, limitations, or impairments. Particularly offensive to me are the terms:

Differently-able
Definitely-able
Handi-capable

First and foremost, people are intrinsically unique. This is the wisdom of the Creator. Within all His creation there exists a broad spectrum of physical abilities and the aforementioned terms serve only to homogenize and lay aside our uniqueness.

My other issue is that these terms are often just plain inaccurate. Point of fact: there are things that I am definitely *not* able to do. Travel with me sometime, and you will see. Differently-abled describes all of us. And I mean all human beings. We are unique creations with different abilities. Why use this to only describe someone with a physical, mental, or emotional challenge, limitation, or impairment? Handi-capable? Someone was drunk when they made up that one.

Here is my bottom line: please don't choose some politically correct term, thinking it is more acceptable. I have dealt with the reality of my body for a long time. You need not find a softer, gentler (in your mind) term to describe me. You are cordially invited to drop, in my presence, the political and/or socially "correct" lingo. I am a physically disabled person who rather likes the term "gimpy." Try smiling when you say "gimpy," it's a great word!

What should I tell you in this chapter of my growing-up years? First, there is the physical stuff, but there is so much of all that. People are often curious about my physical history. I understand because the physical stuff is something to which people may relate. Almost everyone knows someone who has had knee or hip replacement. When I am on the road, and tell the physical history, I build bonds with people. I like that.

And more than just the physical history, there is the emotional road traveled. The disease may affect my bones and joints, but the reality of the disease impacted my psycho/social development. To tell you one part of the story without telling the other is a waste of both our time.

The disease ran a rapid course through my body until about age eight. From my feet and ankles to my neck and jaw, nearly every joint was affected. Both of my elbows quit bending and thus fused themselves at a ninety-degree angle. One of the attributes of my particular brand of arthritis is that it "lead pipes" the joint. Two fingers, one on each hand, stopped growing when I was about five years old. My chubby little fingers have, over the years, become a point of interest for small children. I use them to my advantage when speaking with children, as they love having bigger fingers than I. My right knee was surgically fused (age six, and again at fourteen), as were both of my ankles (age seven). The rest of my body was often stiff and difficult to move. And there were more surgeries, so many more surgeries.

Thankfully, I don't remember the pain. I know I had pain but I cannot recall it in graphic detail. This must be one of God's great gifts. We are not wired to be able to re-experience pain from memory. My friends who have had children say that this is how women are able to go through labor more than once.

Our pediatrician advised my parents to put me in school early. He felt it important for me to think about something other than my health. I was a bright child and to sit around with nothing to do would be detrimental. Once tested, I was allowed to start first grade at age five. And I loved it. Although I couldn't run like the other children, I certainly could read. The classroom was my level playing field.

Growing up, there were two issues that were constantly held in tension and required a real balancing act: school and the arthritis. Decisions in one arena affected the other. Surgery to support my mobility needed to be timed for minimal impact on school attendance. In other situations there was pain and immobility that made being at school impossible. I was not a complainer and did not use my health to avoid physical activity. Still there were situations when the rigors of the day took their toll. The school nurse knew our phone number by heart.

School began for me as a cool place, a place which

I enjoyed, and where I felt comfortable. Perhaps most first-graders like school. I attended a private school with open-air ramadas for classrooms. The playground was amazing. It had a full-sized fire truck and other great things to stimulate the mind and allow for great imaginary play. It was a magical place—everything the hospital was not.

Second grade began with an entirely different school experience. I had surgery during the summer between first and second grade and following surgery developed a life-threatening post-operative staph infection. After over a month in the hospital I wasn't able to begin school with the rest of my classmates. In order to catch up, I began the school year with "homebound" education. My teacher came to our house. She was a nice lady who helped me considerably. Although I loved learning and being the center of one person's attention, I missed the socialization that school provided.

After Christmas I was enrolled in a public school. Not just your average school—Miles Elementary School had classes for children with physical disabilities. We were segregated from the able-bodied kids in our classrooms but shared the cafeteria and the playground. We were a very eclectic bunch. There were kids with hearing aids and others with braces and wheelchairs. My third-grade class picture is a display of the wide spectrum that is our human condition. Our playground battles were about things different than most. We argued about whether the relay race could be run with your leg braces locked or unlocked. FYI—locked is much faster.

The best part of that year and a half was the bus rides to and from school. We, of course, had a bus capable of picking up kids of all physical circumstances. Our driver's name was Bill, and he had an aide named Ernie. They would pull up in front of the house, the lift was lowered, and Ernie rolled my wheelchair and me on. There was always laughter and joking on our bus. Although the bus rides were long (we picked up kids from around the city) it was a happy place to start and end the day.

The surgery that occurred between first and second grade was a procedure to fuse my right leg. This would place my leg in a stable position. It removed all flexion of the knee but allowed me to stand and walk with far less pain. The long-term goal was to limit the disease's destructive fervor and preserve the leg for future medical advances. What those advances would be were unknown to us at the time, but doctors were certain there would be surgical innovations, which would serve me at some time in the future.

The procedure went according to plan until the days immediately post-op when I developed a recurrent spike in fever. The doctors had been (according to my mother) arguing about the cause of my spiking fever.

Of course there is very little of that time that I remember. There are a couple of notable exceptions. First, I recall Dr. Schwartzmann (the orthopedic surgeon) walking boldly into my room. I was coloring. He took a crayon and drew a rectangle on my cast, at the knee area. My anxiety shot up because I knew, from experience, what was coming: the dreaded cast saw. I had a fear of and never liked the cast saw. Even though I had been told (repeatedly) that the saw wouldn't cut anything as soft as skin, I was a child and whether it was the look of the blades or the sound it made, the cast saw always triggered fear and even panic.

Dr. Schwartzmann had drawn and was about to cut a window out of the cast.

Finally, he was going to see what was going on inside the cast. So, he began to cut and I got a serious case of nervous chatter. That's what happened when I was frightened; I prattled on about nothing. As he cut through the plaster and then the underlying bandages, the problem behind the fever became obvious. It was staphylococcus. Once you smell "staph," you never forget it. The smell was rancid, terrible, and intense. What a miserable mess! It was as though there was a canyon where the incision had been made. And that canyon was full of the green, slimy puss, which had literally carved away a portion of my body.

"Staph" is highly contagious, requiring immediate isolation. For nearly a month, isolation kept my germs away from others, and their germs away from me. A secondary infection could have been catastrophic. Mama moved into the hospital and stayed with me. I had my mom but there was something missing. This was the first time I had gone to the hospital without my beloved teddy bear, Ted. He was a gift from Mama and Daddy for my first birthday and my ever-present buddy. I always slept with Ted and he knew all my secrets. In an attempt to be a "big girl" I had chosen to leave Ted at home. That was all well and good until isolation and the extended stay. Ted wasn't able to come into isolation, so I had to be brave without him. I was over forty years old the next time I left Ted at home when going to the hospital.

After a month in the hospital, it was my mother's nursing skills that enabled me to go home sooner than expected. Doctors allowed her to change and redress my wounds. Nobody wanted to be around when she did so because the odor was intense and the wound was scary ugly. The process was nerve wracking, and I whimpered anxiously at the possibility of discomfort. With calm words and her trademark "get the job done" attitude, Mama nursed me back to health. It was not the first time, and it would not be the last.

Our family moved from Tucson to Scottsdale, Arizona, in 1964. My father took a new job as a district manager for a new insurance agency. It was a promotional opportunity that he needed to take. Leaving Tucson, however, meant leaving my very familiar world. My aunt, uncle, and cousins were important in my life; we were growing up together like brothers and sisters. We had lived in a neighborhood without many children, and I had very little experience making friends. My family was the center of my social life. And my physicians were in Tucson. For some time, we drove the two hours in order to continue to see them. We had been through so much together; it was hard to think of life without those doctors.

It was during those trips that my imagination ran wild. Sitting in the car, looking out the windows, I dreamed of being a princess or the president. In all those dreams, and the ones that continue to this day, I am rarely crippled. It is not that I dream of being different than I am, for I know clearly that will not happen this side of heaven. Rather, it has just never been part of my self-image. This is what it is.

Pima Elementary School in Scottsdale was worlds different from Miles. I was now walking on crutches. That was great for me, but physically harder of course than a wheelchair. Stamina was something I needed to develop if I was to have a chance at keeping up with my able-bodied classmates. In all honesty, I was more than a little intimidated. I thought of myself as shy, but truthfully it was a serious lack of self-confidence.

My classmates were also challenged. They had never been around a child on crutches. I was different and therefore scary. Children with disabilities were not "mainstreamed" in those days, so I was a complete novelty to them. That which we do not know or understand, we often fear. This is true for both children and adults.

Staring. There was so much staring. Children are more obvious, but adults stare just as much as the little ones; they simply attempt to hide it. For the majority of my life (and especially in that age) staring has been most upsetting to me. Eyes, when focused on you, can sear the soul like a laser. It is rude, unnecessary, and can be painful. Children should be taught, and adults should know better. (*Stop, Paula—you are beginning to rant!*)

Those early schooldays were tough as I had a hard time making friends. Most nine-year-olds wanted to run and play during recess, not sit and chat with me. Consequently, I often watched, alone, while others played. Suffice to say, recess was not my favorite time of the day.

Physical education (PE) class was nearly as bad. Although I enjoyed being as physically active as possible (always have and still do), there was no way a child on crutches could do a proper jumping jack. Anything that involved getting on the ground was out of the question, because I could not get back up by myself. During those exercises,—the cheese (me)—stood alone. That happened all too often.

In the classroom I was on equal footing with everyone else. I was an above-average reader, but arithmetic was not my strong suit. Teachers treated me fairly and recognized my potential, and thus held me to a high standard. This served me well until children complained that I was "teacher's pet." Looking back, I was likely seen as one of those kids who "kissed up" to the teacher and was therefore distrusted, or at the very least, suspect.

I had a few friends who, over the years, broke through the fear in order to get to know the new/different girl. These girls ate lunch with me. We played "cats in the cradle" with string and even jacks on the playground benches. I felt great comfort when I didn't have to face the school day alone. A couple of them remained friends through high school, college, and beyond. One of my hopes for this book is that they know how important their friendship was to me then. Time and tide have moved us away from one another, but I remain eternally thankful to God for my friends Teri and Rojann.

Over the years, school became a burden; a place I wanted to get in and out of quickly. It was a place where I experienced both emotional and physical distress. I was treated with overt cruelty in varying forms for the five years I was in that school (fourth through eighth grades). Children, when not trained to act otherwise, can be cruel. I understand that when they don't know better, some consideration must be made. But as I write this, I continue to pray for a world where parents will teach their children the grace to encounter differences with sensitivity.

Name-calling was actually the small stuff. Nobody likes to be called cruel names like "four legs" and "weirdo." But, I had great parents who helped me understand that those were only words. "Sticks and stones can break my bones but words can never hurt me" was the mantra I was taught. Most of the time, I was okay. Others, I confess, hurt me mightily.

There was physical abuse as well. There were "accidental" kicks at my crutches, which could cause me to trip and nearly fall. When I lose balance and am heading toward a fall, I cry out. Loudly. Generally, I could and would catch myself, but the kids around me broke into rounds of laughter. Being laughed at, especially as a child, is no fun.

On one particular day, the abuse escalated. It always started the same way. Boys gathered in a circle and the girls grew silent and watched the scenario unfold. One boy would break from the circle and head toward me for the "accidental trip." It was difficult to brace myself, so I generally tried not to move.

On this day I was walking; perhaps I was trying to show bravery or bravado. The boy (I will call him Dylan) came near me and slipped his foot toward my crutches. I tripped and made my usual loud noise, but this time I went all the way to the ground—down onto recently irrigated grass I fell. There was some laughter but most kids simply ran. I was flat on wet ground, and they all ran away. I cried, a lot. Apparently, it wasn't until I was noticed to be missing following recess that an adult came looking for me. The principal came and picked me up. He called my mother who came to school to take me home. The students were punished by after-school detention, which did not have the desired contrition-promoting effect.

This was the low point in my school life. I can vividly recall the discussion with my mother on our way home that day. "I'm not going back," I declared. "Not today, not tomorrow, and not ever." I wasn't going back to school. While I lamented my life, and railed against the challenges of school, Mother listened patiently.

By now we were at home, sitting in the car, parked in our garage. We often had conversations to complete and remained in the car until the appropriate break. She began, as she often did, with "I understand."

I was still upset. "You can't understand; they didn't push you into the water." (Years later I came to understand that they might as well have pushed her; that's what it means to be a mother.)

My mind was set. I was not willing to return to school. Tears were subsiding as the clarity of my decision brought comfort to my aching heart.

"Are you finished?" Her calm tone asking such a deliberate question didn't surprise me. That's her style.

"I guess." Perhaps I was trying to leave open my option for rebuttal.

"Well, I have a question," she began.

"Yeah."

"When did you become so helpless?" She reminded me that I knew how to stand up for myself. "Why are you willing to give up now?"

The rest of the dialogue boiled down to one of my mother's famous pep talks. She was not willing to let me let others get the best of me. She was insistent that I not give up.

By the time my father came home we were out of the car and in the house. My daddy was ready to break a kid's neck, leaving Mama to balance two emotional basket cases. Yet, as the evening came, our family chat concluded with a plan.

The plan was simple. I would return to school with my parents' admonition and blessing to defend myself. They would speak with the principal, informing him that if the school could not protect me, I would protect myself.

I returned to school with a newfound, or perhaps it was rediscovered, sense of self-determination. However, Mother's morning pep talk lasted only through the morning. My return to school was hardly noticed. There was only minimal apology from the students who were forced by teachers to do so. Nobody bothered me. That sounds good, but what it meant was that I was ignored. My friends were kind, but they too risked becoming social outcasts if they spent much time with me. I became invisible, a non-person. This was more painful than the physical trauma, and more hurtful than the teasing and verbal taunts. It was a lonely time for me. There's something sad, really sad, about feeling alone in a crowd. That was my life and all too frequently those days, or memories of those days, carried into my adult consciousness. I distrusted my environment and my peers, which lead to a less-than-full participation in life. My self-confidence was wounded and took years to repair.

For some time, kids left me alone. Whether they were sincerely remorseful or just bored with taunting me, I had a pretty good stretch of days without anything close to physical abuse. My antenna stayed up for any possible attack. If they came near me, I was ready.

The day came. As I saw the boys huddle, I knew the time had come for me to stand up for myself. This time the boy (I will call him Earl) broke from the circle and headed toward me. I knew the timing was critical. When the need presented, I was able to respond. Earl came close and I pulled back one of my crutches and with all my strength I swung the crutch and hit Earl in the shin.

He yelped in pain. I had hit him hard. Years of walking on crutches had given me serious upper body strength. I had taken a full windup and laid the crutch full into his shin. No wonder he yelped.

At least I wasn't laughing at him. And there was noticeable silence from the other little demons. They scattered. It only took that one time for me to change their minds and help them reconsider abusing me. It never happened again. So rather than taunt and abuse me, they ignored me. It was back to the silent treatment. It was not fun, but at least, like my parents said, I was safe.

There is a rather comical follow-up to this incident. Kids were cautious around me, perhaps for fear that I would "go postal" and beat on them. One day, I was sitting (alone) on a playground bench during lunch recess. My crutches were leaning on the bench on either side of me. Watching other kids play was something I did frequently. The sound of the game of tag from behind me didn't cause alarm. Boys chasing boys, nothing new about that.

I was startled when one of them (we will call him Marty) attempted to jump over the bench I was sitting on. His momentum carried him over the bench, but he landed directly on my wooden crutch. The physics must have been perfect because the crutch snapped in half. All of this happened so quickly that it scared both Marty and me. Perhaps he thought of my violent streak and simultaneously realized I still had one good, intact crutch. He dropped to the ground and said, "I'm sorry, please don't hit me." Poor kid.

As the lunch recess bell rang, I picked up my good

crutch and gathered the broken pieces of the other and returned to my classroom. At the end of the school day, I headed toward the parking lot where my mother would be waiting. Another tough day at school would mean a long talk on the short ride home. More time would be spent in the garage.

Today, however, the routine changed. As I began down the long center hallway, I was met by my mother. She was carrying a new pair of crutches. Aluminum crutches. The new ones I had longed for, for some time. I was elated.

I have always been an extrovert, and being with people is a natural part of my personality. Having few friends was hard for a person who wanted to be deep in the social swim. There had always been plenty of people around me; physicians, therapists, and family were no substitute for the friends and social acceptance I really wanted.

As I look back, the first time I can remember being aware of my desire to be part of the social life of my peers was in junior high. Oh, seventh grade! Typing those words just sent shivers down my spine. It was the practice at our school that seventh grade was when school dances began. Held after school, they seem innocent in retrospect. Classmates spoke about the upcoming dance with excited anticipation. News of the first scheduled dance brought the girls around me to the edge of hysteria with chatter about what they would wear and with whom they would dance.

I too caught the fever. A new outfit, I was certain I needed a new outfit. My poor mother suffered my endless pleas for the latest fashion. I needed this new outfit to be like the other girls. Repeating the wardrobe choices I had heard about at school, I insisted that everyone was getting new clothes. I needed this new outfit to be like the other girls'.

I was surprised one afternoon when, upon arrival after school, there was a new dress laid out on my bed. When excited, I scream. Loudly. This time my scream of joy was not just for a new dress. It was for a new dress with matching cloth purse. It was a beautiful red paisley dress with puffy sleeves. But wait—there's more: navy fishnet stockings! I was over the moon. Keep in mind it was 1966.

The following day in school I was able to join in the conversation about new clothes. Secretly, I was certain none could top my dress and stockings, but the girls who were talking about the shoes they were getting for the dance more than intimidated me. Some would be wearing their first pair of high heels and others told of new "go go" boots.

The night before the dance, Mama was helping me bathe and do my hair. We were talking about the dance. I told her of my gratitude for my beautiful new outfit and my sadness about the boots. My feet would never have allowed me to wear either boots or high heels, and I was sad at feeling so obviously different.

Before I could get too emotional or start to cry, my mother changed the subject. "How would you like to shave your legs?" she asked. Shave my legs? YES! It was the first time, and I was delighted. In an instant, the boots and heels were a distant thought. I was going to have my legs shaved! Sometimes it really is the simple joys that the mean the most.

The dance was the following afternoon. I am not sure how the teachers taught anything that day. There were way too many hormones running loose. Most girls could hardly wait to get to the restroom at the end of the school day and change into their dance clothes. I was among the few who wore their dance clothes to school that day. I did so as I was unable to change clothes independently. Others wore them in order to "show off." The social elite labeled all of us as weirdos. This was not the way I wanted the day to begin.

Our dance took place in the school cafeteria/multipurpose room. As we entered, the boys immediately ran to one side of the room and the girls to the opposite side. All of us were a little on edge at this new experience. My anxiety was complicated by the lack of a chair on the girls' side of the room. I could not stand for an entire hour. A teacher (eventually) brought a chair for me. Although I was relieved about the pain of standing, I felt uneasy about the way this separated me from the rest of the girls. Sitting in my chair at the end of the line, I also felt the stares of everyone who noticed I was different.

Alone, I watched as the dancing began. My heart raced as I waited to be asked to dance. One song ended and another began, and still no invitations to dance. Soon a horrible sadness began to take over my spirit. I was alone with the only dance partner I would know: despair. I wanted to cry, but couldn't risk the embarrassment.

As the dance was drawing toward its close, a few of my friends came around. They were eager to share the news of which boy and what song. A couple of my friends seemed to sense that it had been a difficult and long hour for me and tried to offer comfort. "It's okay" and "I'm okay" were the only things I would say.

Then it happened. Looking up I saw one of the boys heading toward me. BC was one of those kids whose body grew much more rapidly than the rest of the boys his age. He was a bit of an oaf and not at all the cool boy of my dreams. But there he was coming toward me.

Indeed, he was there to ask me to dance. His invitation was not at all graceful or charming, yet it was an invitation to dance. I stood up, secured my crutches and walked toward him. It was awkward for both of us.

Before I could reach him, I became abruptly aware of the events in the background. Most of the boys were laughing and pointing fingers. Many of the girls were as well. BC and I had been used for their pleasure. This was not a boy asking a girl to dance. Rather, BC had been "dared" to ask me to dance. A fact he admitted to me years later.

I would not play along with the joke. Returning to my seat I waited for the dance to be over so that I could go home and cry. That was the first and last school dance I attended. I was crushed, disappointed, embarrassed, and confused. Why they would be so cruel wasn't even the first question in my mind. I couldn't understand why no one would ask me to dance. It didn't even dawn on me that my crutches might be a stumbling block. My father (a dance instructor in his early years) had always been able to dance with me; why couldn't one of my classmates? Worse than the actual dance experience, I knew there was nothing I could do to resolve the situation except return to school and hope that the joke would run its sick course.

Many, many years later, I came to understand that the sad girl in the fabulous red dress and navy fishnet stockings was not really alone at the dance. I grew to know that the grief of that day was not mine alone. I was then, as I am now, in the company of a loving God.

A God who loved me enough to send his Son to the dance with me. A Son who promises me that not all dances will be painful. I am on Jesus' dance card. My only sadness now is for that girl sitting alone at the end of the line. I wish she knew then what I know now.

Family was my safe place. With very few school friends and neighbors who were generally younger, I came to rely on my family. I have only one sister, Julie, who is seven years my junior. She wasn't really a playmate. But she was such a cute little kid and generally (for a kid sister) good to have around. As we grew older, we were able to play together somewhat. All I wanted to tell anyone about my relationship with my sister is well represented in a story from those tough elementary school days.

My classmate (and neighbor) invited me to her house to play with Barbie dolls. It was the first invitation to a neighbor's house to play. I was pretty excited. My Barbies were in two "Barbie Cases," a wardrobe shaped like a suitcase and my pride and joy, a fabulous black patent leather hat carrier.

With one case in each hand I took my crutches and headed four houses down the block. Walking that distance was no easy task for me. Walking and carrying those two bags was doubly difficult. Mother watched from our kitchen window. She says she was at once so proud and so sad. Proud that I would do this walk on my own and yet sad to know the pain it cost me.

Finally at my destination, I rang the front door bell. No answer. Rang again; still no answer. Eventually, I understood that either they were not going to answer the door, or there was no one at home. I was suspicious of the first, and tried to believe the latter. Whether there was a miscommunication or evil intent to hurt my feelings, I left feeling sad and dejected.

Home seemed so far away. The Barbie cases felt heavier. Walking was harder because I was crying. The despair I was experiencing made every step more challenging.

Fortunately, Mama looked out the kitchen window and saw me headed home. She told Julie to "go help Paula." Julie was only about three years old and nearly the same size as my Barbie cases.

When I saw my little sister heading toward me, I was overwhelmed. Round-faced and wide-eyed, she came loping toward me. Oh, she was adorable! I was feeling sorry for myself, but it warmed my heart that she was there for me. I shall never forget what she said: "My help you." So cute.

I had never allowed her to touch my Barbies. Older sisters can be pretty mean about keeping the little sister away from the good toys. My previous selfishness did not deter her. She took hold of the Barbie cases, one in each hand, and dragged them back to our house. I trailed behind her.

Once at home, Mama greeted us. Before I could go into a tailspin over being wronged by a supposed friend, Mama had things to say. She wanted me to always remember that the rest of the world may sometimes feel harsh, and that I may indeed get my feelings hurt. "But," she told us, "you each have a sister. You must always take care of each other. And especially when others are unkind, you know you have someone who will always come to your rescue." As always, my mother could find the pony in the deepest horse shit, the hope and promise contained in every situation.

I don't recall exactly how that conversation ended. By then I was crying, and I suspect (like in other similar moments) Julie and I hugged and she said, "Don't cry, Paw-do."

Julie and I grow closer with each passing year. The difference in our age has become inconsequential. There are times in our adult life that we have used the shorthand phrase "May I carry" or "Will you please put down those Barbie cases." No, we don't play with Barbies. But we do have each other's back and are there to come to each other's rescue.

Family finances necessitated Mother's return to work when I was in the seventh grade. She worked for an amazing family physician, Dr. Alden, who became our family doctor. He referred us to a new orthopedic surgeon who became an important part of my future.

Dr. Alden suggested that my parents look into orthopedic shoes for me. My feet had been difficult to fit in shoes for a long time. They were still (and are) wide, flat, and deformed. For years I had worn whatever shoes we could find.

Based upon Dr. Alden's recommendation, mother bought a pair of Oxford-style lace-up shoes. They were in my mind ugly old-lady shoes. Picture old-fashioned nurses' duty shoes in a taupe/khaki color. The hard leather was uncomfortable at first, which contributed to my unwillingness to wear them. I was subjected to enough criticism, I worried that would worsen with the ugly shoes. I can't be certain if it did or not; I was just keenly aware that my shoes were nothing anyone would want to wear.

I've said it before and will again, saying "no" to my mother is futile. She bought the shoes and I was going to wear them. She would win any argument to the contrary. Thank God.

After a little breaking in, the shoes felt comfortable. Not only that, but my feet also started to feel better. Those ugly shoes were supporting my feet. And support meant less pain.

In the weeks and months that followed, there was a real change happening to my body. Those ugly shoes provided the support to do something I hadn't done since I was a very little girl. I began to take steps, around the house, without my crutches. It was miraculous. There is simple pleasure found in simple movement.

One day in the spring of eighth grade I chose to go to school without my crutches. It was nerve-racking. I worried about all manner of things like: what if I get tired? What if I need to go to the restroom more than the normal number of times? There were lots of "what ifs" but the pep talk from my family inspired me to give it a shot. The day was a success as I made it through without using crutches. There would be more test days with great results and a growing confidence. On April 26, 1969, I declared myself to be "off the sticks."

Those ugly shoes liberated me. Liberated may seem an odd word. Walking on crutches is by no means the worst fate that could befall a person. I did pretty well on them. In those days I considered the crutches far preferable to a wheelchair. But crutches are challenging. It is difficult to hold or carry anything while on them. And they absolutely chew up my armpits. Now, if you are a purist, you know that the crutches aren't supposed to really touch your armpits—certainly not while weight bearing. The proper way to use crutches is to use your forearms to hold yourself up (off the armpits); however, I have no hand, wrist, or forearm strength. So, I literally hang on the crutches. Consequently, my armpits were (and are still a bit now) hamburger.

I was really liberated to live a more "normal" life. When time came for our graduation ceremony, I walked, like all the rest of my classmates, to receive my certificate. My name was called and the number of people who were cheering and applauding for me as I crossed the stage startled me. I could not understand why. I had never been a popular kid, and so it was a surprise for me to hear the crowd's exuberance.

After the ceremony I was anxious to see my parents. When we found one another, there were still tears in both Mama and Daddy's eyes. "Did you hear them cheering for me" I asked.

"We sure did," Mama answered. They yelled, "Go Paula—Go Paula."

We were all quite emotional. It was a wonderful moment in my life. It was also a moment that my parents were not certain would ever happen. The story they had never told me was shared in the days following graduation. The fact that they didn't know I would live to this age was shocking to me. Furthermore they had even been advised early on to consider institutionalizing me. So this night of real normalcy was indeed cause for celebration.

Perhaps the singularly most important moment in my growing up years occurred when I was in high school. My new orthopedic surgeon, Dr. Howard Aidem, offered a brand-new procedure. It was a procedure that would radically improve my quality of life.

I spoke earlier about the way that my elbows had "lead-piped," frozen at about a ninety degree angle, when I was between five and six years old. This meant that I had not been able to wash my own hair and face. It made for all sorts of personal care and dressing issues. Button-front blouses (far more common in those days) were nearly impossible. Now that I was a teenager, my need for independence was becoming more urgent. So when he offered this still somewhat experimental procedure to replace my elbow joint with a prosthetic joint, thus allowing for movement, we jumped at the opportunity. It was a leap of faith. But my whole life had been an act of faith.

The surgery was not at all like any of my subsequent joint replacements. I was casted and held immobilized for fifteen weeks. There was high anxiety as we sat in the doctors' waiting room on the day that the cast was removed. We always waited for this doctor. But this particular day we waited what seemed like an eternity. Mama and I had done this so many times, but my daddy was not a patient waiter. As it turned out, I was the last patient seen that day.

At long last we were in a room. Dr. Aidem walked quickly and purposefully. He entered the room and immediately (and without any chit-chat) began removing the cast. This was a great unveiling for all of us, my parents, the doctor and me. With our breath held, he lifted my arm from the cast and it bent! We all cried.

Years earlier, Dr. Schwartzmann had said that artificial joints would come. I was now living in that future. My arm bent, but not all the way. I got about thirty-degrees range of motion. My surgeon was disappointed, but I was not. For the first time in my memory, my arm bent and there was nothing disappointing about that. More specifically, I could touch my face. My hand moved rapidly from one part of my face to another. My finger went from my mouth to picking my nose. *(I hope it went in that order!)* Scratching my forehead and playing with my hair, I did it all. If you have ever seen Patty Duke's brilliant portrayal of the young Helen Keller, you may have a sense of what those moments in the doctor's office were like. Just as the recognition of the word "water" brought Helen to explore for new words—this was Paula wanting to experience touching the parts of her that had been out of her reach.

It's all a bit comical, looking back. How silly I must've looked. But it really was a life-changing moment, and I could not help myself. I could now do my own hair, button my blouse, put on makeup, and pick my nose. These are more than important. I cried tears of joy. So did my parents. So did the doctor.

That elbow replacement would be followed by another (four years later) that did not work at all. The arm would not bend. A year later we tried again and this time got the hoped-for result of about a forty degree range of motion. Again, not full motion, but functional enough to be worthwhile. Two working elbows was such a revelation.

During grade school, when I grew weary and complained about my circumstance, Mama told me that high school would be better. She said that when children matured, things would change. She was right. I was never one of the popular kids, but I did have a few more friends. My self-confidence began to gradually improve.

In the years of late high school and college, the active disease went into a bit of a remission. My pain and stiffness were much less problematic. It was a glorious time of feeling free from much of the pain, and less limited by the stiffness and immobility of years past.

My parents were always looking for ways for me to experience life "normally." If they could they would (and did) provide opportunities for me to do things that other kids did. I spent time in scouting and then became a Camp Fire Girl *(Wo-He-Lo)*, including summer camps and camping trips. Mama and Daddy loved amusement parks. Whether it was the local park, a fair, or the biggies like Disneyland, we went with fun as priority one. Never looking at what I could not ride, we looked with excitement for what I could. When I was too big for them to lift me onto a carousel horse, they made it fun for me to ride on the benches.

We were on vacation following one of my toughest surgeries. A family visit to Denver included a visit to Elitch Gardens. I remember it as beautiful. I also remember (likely because of the many stories told in the years that followed) that the amusement park staff were so very kind and gracious to me. Front of the line, multiple rides, and all without charging any tickets for me to ride. I was treated like a princess.

Growing up gimpy was not an easy ride on a magic carpet. There were plenty of tough times. But they weren't all bad. Yes, I have a tough disease that has made for some very difficult moments. There have been challenges for sure. And sometimes the pain can really cloud the retrospective lens.

My personality has formed around the concept of hope. Where many people might see darkness, I look to find, even cling to, any kernel of light. As a consequence, I have found this a tough chapter to write. I wanted to be honest about the reality of growing up gimpy. At the same time I didn't want to invite pity or sadness. I have had an awesome life, filled with wonderful experiences.

The purpose of this chapter was to share some of the critical points along the early part of my journey. Please, do not cry for me because of the challenges I have faced. Laugh with me through the memories I share—some of them are much funnier looking back. And give thanks along with me, for a mighty God who has traveled this journey with me.

We all have history, a past that has shaped us and informed our present and our future. Not all of our history can be judged as entirely good or bad. Do you remember learning this phrase in school? "If we do not learn from the past, we are doomed to repeat it." For some of us, it is nearly impossible to let our past remain in the past. We may seek ways to relive our "better days." Or we may cling to hurts, which can cripple our ability to live a happy present.

I have said that writing this book has been challenging for me. If you were going to write your autobiography, would it be a challenge for you to examine your personal history? There are questions that would provide the beginning. Questions such as: What is your greatest joy—or the high point of your life? What were the circumstances around the lowest point in your life? Which event has the most powerful impact on you today, and why? If you choose to spend time reflecting on where you have been—don't forget to celebrate and look forward as well.

Good and gracious God,
Our precious and abiding Lord,

Scripture tells us that we are
curiously and wondrously made.
Grant us we pray,
the lens of grace to see ourselves as You see us.
Allow us to recognize within our history
Your abiding presence.
Inspire us to look forward
in full recognition that we
keep company with You on this journey of life.

Amen

5

The Parts In-Between

"Yada Yada Yada"

This book was never intended to be a precisely chronological autobiography. My intention was to highlight some of the crucial moments in my journey. During the editorial process, I conceded that it may be helpful to fill in some of the gaps along the way. YADA YADA YADA (a phrase popularized in the classic TV sitcom *Seinfeld*) seemed the perfect subtitle. It is wonderful shorthand to skip through some of the less critical parts of the story.

Up to this point, I have shared what I consider to be the launching pad for the events to come. You now know of my diagnosis and the challenges of growing up with a painful and deformed body. You also know that I have been not only exposed to faith but also nurtured in it by a loving family. These two points are the foundation upon which the rest of the story is built.

I graduated from high school in 1973 and enrolled at Arizona State University in the fall of that same year. Just as high school was better for me than grade school,

I hoped the same would be said of college. Joining a community of forty-thousand-plus students and faculty felt a bit daunting. In order to mitigate some of the isolation that can all too readily come from being a small fish in a very big sea, I chose to participate in sorority Rush Week. I had hopes of finding a community within the larger community.

Following one of my mother's famous pep talks and with my own strong desire to overcome low self-confidence issues, I headed into a week of the unknown. Few of my high school friends were attending ASU and none were participating in Rush Week. This would be a solo venture. Needless to say, I was nervous in the extreme.

Rush Week participants were housed in the dormitory adjacent to the sorority dormitory. Once unpacked, I waited for my roommate to arrive. It would be good to have someone to talk to about the process, and I was anxious to meet her. I fantasized that she and I might join the same sorority and become lifelong friends. She, however, never arrived. I never knew if she simply backed out of Rush Week or if she found another roommate. I was left saddened and the specter of being alone contributed to the rise in my anxiety meter.

Each day of Rush Week, participants were invited to attend a series of parties. These were sales rallies where both the sorority and the potential pledges marketed themselves one to another. In two days, we attended a party for every sorority. After that point, the sororities that have an interest in you issued return invitations. Some girls received invitations to all and had to make decisions on which they accepted. At this point Rush Parties turned into beauty pageants as each day the competition grew and the wardrobe became more formal. This invitation process repeated through the week until the final night when there were only two (very formal) parties, following which invitations to join were extended and final decisions were made.

Everyone was invited to all of the parties on the first two days. In the days that followed there was excitement to check mailboxes each morning to discover whether invitations were there. Rush Week participants may receive invitations from all of the sororities and must immediately choose which to accept, as there were a limited number of parties that may be attended each day.

I did not have that problem as I was invited back to only three. I was crestfallen. Rejected by nine was a tough pill to swallow. It was all I could do to muster the courage to go out of my room and tell the others that I was only attending three parties. I was embarrassed. In an odd sort of way, it was a relief that most of them were so self-absorbed that they didn't care about what invitations I did or did not receive. After a call and cry with my mother, I pulled myself together and attended the three parties. Casting a hopeful light on my situation was all I knew to do. After all, I wasn't out. Yet.

That came very early the next morning. The Rush Leader for my floor knocked on my door at five a.m. to inform me that I had no invitations in the mailbox. She was there to let me know so that I could pack and leave before the rest of the girls awoke, and so that I might avoid embarrassment. She and another leader quickly stripped my bed, packed my clothing and toiletries, and loaded my car. In less than twenty minutes, my Rush Week experience was over.

Tearfully, I drove home to my mother and grandmother. Home. I needed to be at home. No invitation was required.

They hugged me and cried with me. They loved me back into shape. Ten days later, I was ready to head back to the campus for the start of the school year. Then it was okay to be part of a big campus. In my heart, I hoped I would never see any of those girls again.

Inasmuch as I had not declared a major when I enrolled, a general liberal arts study was where I began. In ensuing years I majored in history, Spanish, secondary education, and finally psychology. Pre-med and nursing were even on the list, albeit briefly. I loved everything about school except mathematics. My hard-core right brain made mathematics the hardest hill to climb. Aside from my propensity for changing majors, my college career was uneventful. There were professors from whom I learned a great deal, not just about their particular subject matter but about life in general. There were times when my health was a stumbling block to timely completion of appointed studies. Perhaps all of the above help to explain why I was on the six-year college plan.

Academics aside, issues of self-confidence, particularly in social situations, continued. Perhaps my childhood wounds were deeper than I recognized. Maybe my small circle of friends left no room for building new relationships. Whatever the reason, I was never comfortable going into a situation where I knew only a few people. I experienced a great internal conflict between my extroverted nature and my growing social anxiety. Social anxiety is not even an accurate term.

I tried to tell myself I was simply shy. Shy sounds so much nicer, maybe somewhat dignified, clearly ladylike. Truthfully, I lacked self-confidence. It took therapy (years later) for me to see the reality of my poor self-confidence. In college I was only beginning to understand this issue. Clarity began to come to me as a result of an incident in my fifth year at ASU.

I was taking a night class in communications. A night class was not my first choice, rather the advice of a professor. The professor told me I would find myself in the company of adult learners with course content better suited for working (or soon to be) professionals. Having already spent four years searching for a career, I looked forward to this class.

The class turned out to be all that I hoped for and more. It was a good mix of working people returning to university to complete a career, and upperclassmen that had delayed taking this required course. Our instructor understood that the course carried with it the onerous "required element" moniker and sought to make the class relevant and enjoyable. Within the first week he had us converted to the joy of public speaking.

Wednesday evening was my favorite time of the week. The topics were stimulating and the instructor motivating. This was not just my perspective. Most of the people in the class arrived early; a sure sign that something good was happening. People were kind and supportive of one another as we all worked together to hone our communication skills.

As with most night classes, we had a long break midway through our three hours together. Those breaks were great for getting to know people and exercising my limited social talents. Casual acquaintances were built, and I enjoyed spending time with several people. One evening, during our break, a couple of those guys told about a party they were planning for the coming weekend. To my delight, and frankly to my amazement as well, they invited me. An immediate rush of adrenaline may account for the missing memory of anything that happened the remainder of that evening.

This is what I do remember of the days following the class and leading up to the party. First, I was so excited, so excited that I bought a new sweater. Looking good was and still is important to me.

My other memory is fear. Seems silly to say I was afraid of a party. More accurately I was afraid of the unknown. I had no experience with social settings outside my small circle of high school girlfriends. I was over twenty-one years old, but a party such as that was new territory to me.

Physical challenges like sitting and standing complicated everything else I was feeling. Although I was able to walk with relative ease, standing could only be done in short stints. Sitting was good but highly dependent on the kind of seat and its height. Beanbag and papasan chairs (popular in the seventies) were the most difficult. With one fused leg and very little mobility and strength in my arms, those chairs were traps. Once in them, I found them almost impossible to escape on my own. If I sat in anything low to the ground, it meant I would need help from someone to stand.

"I would need help from someone." Writing those words brought a rush of emotions and tears to my eyes. Asking for help was so difficult. It would be easy to blame the difficulty on a concern that someone would pull too hard and I would get hurt. It has happened. Kindhearted folks have "helped" me and it has hurt me.

In reality, I disliked asking for help, because it meant the arthritis would be in focus. Asking for help meant I would be seen and known for what I couldn't do. I desperately wanted to be seen for my personality and character rather than the limitations of my physical appearance. I feared being rejected for the one thing I could not change.

Through all the emotional turmoil, my prayers were for strength of spirit, that God would make it easier for me to go to a party. In those days, my faith was something exercised in only the most basic, even childlike manner. I prayed to the God that my mother had promised. Beyond those prayers, I had no awareness of the real strength to be realized in a mature understanding of Jesus. Sadly, the truth of St. Paul's writing in his letter to the Philippians 4: 13 (NRSV): *I can do all things through Christ who strengthens me,* would not be real for me for several more years.

All of my angst could not stop the inevitable. Saturday arrived. My nerves were oddly calmed by, of all things, my new sweater. It was a beautiful wrap cardigan in heathery shades of green and pink. I kept busy getting ready and completing my mental checklist:

- hair—okay—parted down the middle (it was the seventies)
- makeup—simple, yet good
- clothing—sweater is great, but jeans would have been better than my dress slacks
- breath—outstanding

Focusing on that checklist proved the necessary distraction from the anxiety.

During the fifteen-minute drive from my home in Scottsdale to the apartment complex in Tempe, Arizona, anxiety overtook reason. By the time I arrived in Tempe, I was a nervous, anxious mess. Questions bounced around in my head. What if there is no place to sit? What if I'm dressed inappropriately? What if those guys didn't really want me to come to their party? Nervousness morphed into a pathological social anxiety when those "what if" questions began to have "I'm sure" answers. I'm sure there won't be a place to sit because everyone stands at a party. I'm sure the invitation was only to be nice; they didn't think I would really show up. I'm sure I'm overdressed; I look like a middle-aged file clerk going to a Tupperware party. I should have worn jeans.

Rather than park my car and walk into the party, I drove around and around and around. Two hours later, I went home having never set foot at the party. All the rationalization in the world couldn't make the invitation real. I just could not bring myself to go into the apartment complex.

The following week in class, a couple of people asked, "Where were you on Saturday? We missed you at the party." I was embarrassed and ended up lying to these folks, telling them that "something came up." Mine had been the thoughts and actions of a depressed person. It was time to get help.

I find it sad to look back on those times, and my heart breaks for the young woman I was. Overcoming low self-esteem is an ongoing part of my personal journey. In the current day, my strength comes from knowing that the Lord himself has confidence in me. His confidence was demonstrated so long ago in the life of Jesus. When God is for us, shouldn't we be as well? I do not wish to dwell on my mental health issues. I share this experience because I believe I am not the only person to have faced such a demon. If you have, I pray you find the light capable of slaying that darkness.

There came a point at which I chose to leave college rather than pursue the necessary post-graduate training to become a clinical psychologist. School fatigue was, I believe, an unintended consequence of the six-year plan. Reassessing my career goals before committing to a six-year graduate school program was in order. I was ready to work and make some money. The choice was clear.

The decision to postpone graduate school meant I needed to find a job. The hospital seemed the perfect place to apply. Growing up in hospitals and around all kinds of medical professionals left me fluent in the language of healthcare. Samaritan Health Services owned and operated a number of hospitals in the Phoenix metropolitan area and the rural areas of Arizona and southern Utah. I applied for a clerical position at the largest facility, Good Samaritan Hospital. Although I did not get the first job for which I interviewed, I eventually was hired at the corporate personnel office. The work was an ideal fit for me and thus my career in human resources began and my aspiration for a PhD in psychology faded.

Throughout college and my early years in the working world, I was away from the church. I did not overtly reject the faith; rather, it just wasn't a part of my daily life. I knew God loved me, yet I spent very little energy showing my love for Him. I was not a part of a faith community and I didn't do anything in service to someone else. My Bible gathered dust on the shelf, and my prayer life was inconsistent at best. I had no idea what I was missing. Truly, my faith was empty.

Some memories bring joy and others evoke sadness. Writing this transition chapter forced me to recall some pretty tough times. Times I would truthfully rather forget. They weren't any fun then and they aren't much better today.

I have occasionally shared some portions of this chapter in speeches. It has been a revelation to me the difference between speaking the story and writing the story. Writing this story has led me into some of the most emotionally intense portions of my life story. The passage of time brings with it the fading of memory. Writing an autobiography puts one in opposition to this reality. In so many instances, the harder I work to remember the story, the deeper I must dig into the feelings that accompany the events. Honesty of emotion has been a daunting task.

There is a certain ease that comes when speaking the story. I don't believe I intentionally guard myself from sharing the fullness of my experience. Rather, there must be a degree of emotional separation that occurs in the presence of larger groups. I consider my public speaking to be a gift. First, God has gifted me with the ability to stand before audiences with confidence, and proclaim His grace as it is revealed through my journey. Secondly, as I speak, I wish to be in service to my audience. It is from this second point that I derive the intention to set aside my own emotions. It is by the grace of God that I am able to do so. Holding my emotions allows my audience to experience their own emotions.

The crucial thing about those emotions is that they need not have any power in my life now. All the pain is in the past. The person I was then, the road traveled (bumps and all), and even the pain (physical and emotional) are what make me the person I am today. It is through the grace and mercy of our loving God that we are able to leave the past in the past. It is by that same grace and mercy we move forward. I love these words from Hebrews 12:1–2: *Therefore, since we are surrounded by such a great cloud of witnesses, let us throw off everything that hinders and the sin that so easily entangles. And let us run with perseverance the race marked out for us, fixing our eyes on Jesus, the pioneer and perfecter of faith. For the joy set before him he endured the cross, scorning its shame, and sat down at the right hand of the throne of God.*

Time to roll on.

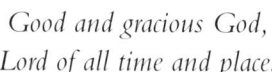

*Good and gracious God,
Lord of all time and place,*

*Sometimes our recollection of the past
leads to deep introspection
and not only a re-memory of those times
but also a re-experience of the pain
associated with those moments.
By your grace and mercy
we place those memories and their pain
into your strong hands.
Open your hands to reveal that they are
now nothing more than dust.
And then transform our focus to gratitude
for the life and love we have in you.*

Amen

6

What I Found in Texas

So many nights I sit by my window
Waiting for someone to sing me his song
So many dreams I kept deep inside me…

> "You Light Up My Life"
> sung by Debbie Boone

So how did a nice Presbyterian girl like me end up in a Lutheran Church? In keeping with Presbyterian theology, I might say that I was "predestined" to become a Lutheran. The doctrine of predestination has long been a cornerstone of Presbyterian theology. *(Who am I kidding? I'm not a theologian and I don't even play one on TV.)*

All kidding aside, the doctrine of predestination, in its most emphatic form, says that everything in our lives is a part of God's plan. If that is indeed the case, then it would stand to reason that God planned all along for me to be a Lutheran. Whether or not, referencing the doctrine of predestination always brings a laugh in my speeches. Sometimes that laugh takes the form of a nervous giggle from the former Presbyterians who are in my mostly Lutheran audiences.

Talking about God's Plan is, for me, like venturing out into the really deep water. The best I can say on this subject is a paraphrase of a sign that hangs in my office. It says: "I do not know the master plan, but I know the Master and that is good enough for me."

Given my unconventional life path, it should come as no surprise that my faith journey began anew after I attended an intensely secular self-help seminar in Texas. In the 1980s, many of my generation were engaged in some sort of quest for personal awareness. Books, workshops, and seminars abounded. From Transactional Analysis to Eastern mysticism, everyone it seemed was turning inward. If you wanted help, you could find it around every corner.

Although I'm sure I was not, I liked to think I was different. I was not a recovering hippie. I did not have a problem finding satisfaction in my work. I was not an emotional basket case looking for some sort of fix for my life. My life was fine, really, just fine. I was twenty-six years old with a decent job and a family that loved me. What more could I wish for? Turns out I was just like many twenty-six-year-olds of my day. I wanted more. More friends, more love, more money, more adventure, and more of something intangible that I did not even recognize at the time.

The 1980s were a time when my own search for a sense of meaning and purpose kicked into a higher gear. I was not alone. Many of my generational peers struggled with the complex and nuanced issues of personal identity and self-worth. We were, after all, living in the most inwardly focused of times. All of us behaved as though we were members of a one-note band; you could have called us the "Me-Me-Me" generation.

I have shared in earlier pages that I was raised to have faith. Singing "Jesus Loves Me" and saying my prayers, at that point, were the extent of my faith maturation. So, it should come as no great surprise that, although I knew of God's love, I did not see the church, or even my faith, as the place to find identity or purpose. I was like so many others who were searching, searching for something, even if we could not articulate what that something was.

My search took me to Texas. Actually, I'm getting ahead of myself. It began in the office of my friend Joel. I was there for a meeting regarding our hospital's employee recognition banquet. Joel Baker was the best florist and party designer (in my completely unbiased opinion) in town. His designs were creative, outrageous, beautiful, and, in a word, fabulous.

My first encounter with Joel had been a few years earlier in his very first shop. He had purchased the shop from a friendly old flower-child hippie. I liked to go into the hippies' old flower shop in the afternoon because I liked the guy and he would sell his flowers at half price. "Share the love—flower power, man." The place was a dump but cheap flowers were irresistible.

One fateful day, I walked into my little old flower shop to find it transformed. No longer a sweet little dump with cheap flowers; it was now an elegant floral boutique. Instantly I knew my daisies were going up in price. Joel, the best looking man I had ever met, greeted me with his beautiful smile, charming personality, and that adorable Texas accent. We hit it off instantly. Combining his charisma with a drive for business excellence led him from that original shop to bigger design studios and the top of society's A-list. He no longer did just parties; he did balls, grand charity balls.

With his amazing success, he still had time and a genuine interest in helping me plan this party. The employee recognition banquet was no ordinary party. The CEO of our hospital had very high expectations. He wanted it to be a really special night for our honorees. Being able to use Joel for this party made my life so much easier. I knew his part would be perfect.

So there we sat in Joel's office. It was always fun to be together, yet I noticed something different about him that day. He glowed. He was at ease. He appeared to be genuinely happy. So obsessed was I with what I was seeing in Joel that I was barely aware of our debate over lilies versus roses. Finally, unable to control myself any longer, I blurted out, "Something's going on with you—something is different—what is it?"

My colleague from the public relations department shrunk into her chair with embarrassment. She told me later that she thought I had lost my mind. Why in the world would I ask such a question?

Joel on the other hand smiled and said, "Girl, where do I start?" He went on to tell me that so much had been happening, really wonderful and amazing stuff. He had been dying to tell me about this fabulous experience. And of course, it was in Texas. He went on to explain just enough about the seminar he had attended to leave me begging for details: amazing people, awesome experiences, plus plenty of Tex-Mex food. All of it had left him with a renewed attitude about life.

"Focused," "happy," and "on purpose" were some of the words he used in explaining his new outlook on life. I knew immediately that I wanted what he now had. *There, I thought, that's what I need in my life. I must go to Texas.*

Joel cautioned that it wasn't that simple, but if I wanted he would assist me in getting there.

The story between that meeting and the day I walked into the conference room of the hotel in Austin, Texas, is lengthy and much better suited to the spoken word. If you ever see me in an airport terminal waiting for a flight, come on over, and I will tell you the rest of the story.

Suffice to say that I went to Texas in search of that something missing from my life. Our small merry band had left Phoenix full of hope and excitement for whatever the next five days would hold. We walked into the conference/meeting room to find our chairs in a semi-circle and a handful of very well dressed people standing around the room. They were a stiff and sober looking lot and I was soon concerned that we would not be having the fun we had all anticipated. Joel was right; it wasn't that easy.

The seminar was led by a trainer (named David) and a team of small group leaders. It began quickly and was more intense than I could have imagined. David was direct and, initially, quite intimidating. I was nervous around him and not at all certain that this was going to yield the same kind of result for me as it had for my friend Joel.

Experiential training (such as this) is unique to each individual. Although challenging, I eventually came to appreciate it all. I learned much about myself and gained clarity about life. My personal purpose and vision for the future began to form.

Many of the lessons I learned are incorporated into the teaching I do today. Although it was an entirely secular seminar, I am amazed by the godly nature of so many aspects of the experience. Personal accountability, the importance and power of forgiveness, and the reality that each individual's life has a unique purpose, are just some of the things around which the training was formed.

Years later, I invited David and his business partner Duane to lead a similar process adapted for the management staff of the hospital where I was the Vice President of Human Resources. The training and its lessons were valuable in that place as well.

Back at the training, I found the something missing from my life. Looking around the room on that first day, my eyes caught a glimpse not of the something, rather someone. In that moment I saw what I am convinced God *(He was involved)* wanted me to see. I saw a BLOND, BLUE-EYED, BIG AS TEXAS LUTHERAN!

Jeff was his name. In the beginning, all that I knew of the blond blue-eyed teddy bear was his name. It wasn't until after the five days (he had been part of the leadership team and socializing with participants was a "no no") that our friendship began. We talked regularly. I traveled to Texas to work on leadership teams and attend graduate retreats. During those times, Jeff and I grew closer and closer. And our phone bills grew larger and larger. Remember, this was way before cell phones.

God raised the ante in our relationship when Jeff shared with me that he was considering a major change in his life. We were having one of our regular lengthy phone conversations. It was the only way to stay connected living in two different states. Truthfully, my hope was that his big change was either to move to Arizona or, better yet, to ask me to marry him. I had fallen, fallen hard for my Texas Teddy Bear. And yes, in that ridiculous girly fashion, I had occasionally practiced writing my married name. Okay—there were even some bridal magazines in my car. My emotions were running faster than my conversation with Jeff.

Curbing my enthusiasm, I chose to be fully present and listen (like a good wife would) and asked, "What's on your mind?"

"I think that God is calling me into the ministry," he said.

"Really (I sighed internally), I wasn't aware that was on your mind." I nearly dropped the phone.

"Oh yes, on and off for some time."

"I guess we have never talked about this before." I was running out of things to say. All I really wanted to say was "what the hell do you mean?" My concern was entirely for myself. Could he be planning on becoming the kind of minister that cannot marry? Yikes!

As I look back on the confusion of that moment, I am once again keenly aware of God's fine hand at work. My next question was to be life changing for me. "What kind of minister do you want to become?"

"Lutheran," he said. "I'm surprised I hadn't told you that before."

Me too, I thought. "Great" is what I said. I had known him to be a man of faith; I just did not know the specifics. I found out many months later about the Lutheran reluctance to speak publicly about their personal faith.

Thankfully, our conversation was soon over. My

memories of the remaining time on the phone are faded. I do, however, remember feeling obsessed with one thing and one thing only. I needed to find a Lutheran church. Fast!

I was a Presbyterian, and knew very little of Lutherans. Mostly I thought of them as "Catholic-light," with aerobic worship (lots of standing up and sitting down) yet without beads.

God must have laughed as he walked with me through this process. There I was investigating this church thing of Jeff's. Little did I know at the moment how God was leading me home.

How did I choose a Lutheran church for my look see? Still hoping for a wedding, I chose to attend a pretty church. Something older, with limestone that would be beautiful for wedding pictures, is what I wanted.

It was early December, a time I now understand as Advent, when I entered my first Lutheran Church. It was as beautiful on the inside as on the outside. Stained glass, beautiful wooden appointments, and an amazing organ made me glad I had chosen this for my visit. It would be perfect for the wedding. A lovely tree was up front with lights, but very few decorations. The place felt like church and for a moment my heart was comforted. I could marry a Lutheran pastor. Whew!

This comfort was short-lived. I had arrived early to be able to get a feel for the place and choose a good seat. Turns out finding a place to sit would not be a problem. There were only a few people in attendance. Very few. Most of them sitting in the back.

Upon closer look, this was an older crowd. Now I was no youngster, but I was probably half the age of the next youngest worshipper. This was a congregation at a turning point; although sadly, no one appeared to be tending to the steering wheel.

Oh, how I wish I could write of the glorious nature of this experience. Sadly, I cannot. Energy level in the room was nil. The only real excitement came when the organist cranked up a lively introduction to the last verse of the hymn. Age, I came to learn later, had very little to do with the atmosphere in that parish. Some "senior" congregations are livelier than younger congregations.

Don't even get me started on the challenge of learning to navigate through the "green book." The green book, properly termed the *Lutheran Book of Worship* (LBW) was the handbook for worship used in those days. It contained liturgies, litanies, prayers, and hymns. To the seasoned Lutheran, it was a much beloved companion in the worship. But to a neophyte such as I, it was impossible to find the proper pages in a timely manner, and "keep up" in the worship.

Driving home was rough, as I was crestfallen and fully into a Scarlet O'Hara kind of moment. "Where could I go—what would become of me?" My visions of being married to Jeff seemed less appealing. Should not the church be a more joyful or at least warmer experience? What the heck is wrong with a church that doesn't sing Christmas carols in mid-December? What was I going to say to Jeff? Lutherans are lifeless, is what I thought. That seemed so mean but I wasn't prepared to lie to him.

STOP—DON'T PANIC!

There was no need to make a rash judgment. I was reminded that there are other Lutheran churches. Having chosen my first church for its appearance, perhaps a more reasoned approach was in order for choosing the next one. And so it was, with that in mind, I chose to visit a congregation closer to my home.

Prince of Peace Lutheran Church was the place. Much closer to home, it seemed a likely church that my Lutheran high school classmates would have attended.

Remembering the challenge of navigating the green book, I arrived early once again. Thankfully. The immediate difference in the two churches was obvious, as this one was packed. What a difference that made. I soon discovered the reason why.

Prince of Peace was in the midst of a very emotional transition. They were saying goodbye to their founding pastor, Phil. He was leaving after nearly thirty years to serve a congregation in California. Many of them were losing the only pastor they had known. He knew them all: happy marriages, rocky relationships, their children, and finances. Their love for him was palpable. Sad on the one hand, and yet all were celebrating this man they adored and praying him Godspeed.

The energy in the room was overwhelming. I found myself feeling a bit disappointed that I had not been a part of this family. It was his next to last Sunday; thankfully I could come back next week to see the end of the story.

The next week was even better. The only issue was the fellow sitting next to me; he was odd. He spent most of the worship reading the Bible rather than participating. At one point this fellow looked at me and said, "This is a good place and you should be here." Like I said, he seemed odd.

Pastor Phil ended his service there surrounded by love. *Maybe I could be a pastor's wife. That*, I thought, *would*

WHAT I FOUND IN TEXAS 83

be the end of it. But as the week passed, I found myself wondering about Prince of Peace. I remembered the young pastoral couple that was still there. What were they like? What would it feel like at Prince of Peace without Pastor Phil?

Sunday came and I was putting on pantyhose and heading back to church. I was going just to check out that clergy couple. The crowds were smaller, but the spirit of the place seemed "right." I don't remember whether it was Scott or Melissa who preached on that day. But at the end of the service, I determined that I would return the following week to hear the other preach.

The Holy Spirit of God was at work. I was in worship every week thereafter. Seems that what I thought I found in Texas was actually to be found closer to home.

Mine was not the conversion marked by hands raised in praise or hallelujah moments. But you probably knew that. You had to have known that from the moment you first read that I am a Lutheran. Grounded in Scandinavian stoicism and German piety, there is just no need for excessive displays—even if those are excessive displays of faith. "Passing the peace" and handshaking is even a bit too much for some in our faith tradition.

> Confessional moment:
>
> I was part of a young adult group that had recently been on retreat. At the retreat center we had shared space at the camp with a large women's group from an Assembly of God Church. At meals, they raised their hands in

praise and thanksgiving. Our pastor remarked that he wouldn't have that sort of display in "his church." He probably should not have said that to a group of still somewhat rebellious young people.

The following Sunday, our congregation welcomed new members. Several of the new members were young adults and were sponsored by those of us who had been on retreat. We sat toward the back. Now, you must know we weren't in the last row because those seats belong to the people who have occupied them for years and who arrive early to make certain the uninformed visitor does not take their seats. Our group had co-opted the newbies into joining our escapade. So, when the prayers of the church were concluded with the traditional Congregational spoken response of Amen—we (all nine of us) did the wave. But only once—we wouldn't want to be too showy, you know.

Actually, conversion is not really the right word to use either. Mine was more of a "drift" into the church. I had a small faith. But just like the stone that rolls down the hill and gathers moss, my small faith grew and grew. It grew from the small seeds planted by my mother and nurtured with love and prayer.

Remember when Glenda the Good Witch tells Dorothy in the *Wizard of Oz* that the answer was with her all along? Searching far and wide, although romantically alluring, is often futile. Answers are close, and it is up to us to pause and look.

The promise of God in my life had been made long

ago. My mother's promise was still in effect. It had been with me all along.

The moment my focus was shifted from *seeking* to *appreciating*, my life changed dramatically. Realizing that God was at work in me brought clarity. The love of Jesus became the joy of my life. And my first steps down the road of discerning God's purpose and calling on my life began.

I couldn't explain the mechanics of how this all occurred, and that fact troubled me a bit. Faith was, I supposed, the answer. Somehow my faith had been stirred up. In that moment, I was content to have the rekindled relationship with Jesus. My seeking and searching was rewarded with something most unexpected, and for which I am eternally grateful. Sometimes searching brings real value into our lives. Understanding might come one day. Yes, perhaps one day I would "get it." But that's for another chapter.

Under the heading of "Where are they now?"…

I am grateful to Joel for his love and friendship. He is back in his beloved Texas doing the work he loves. As delightful as ever, he continues to use his irrepressible spirit and talent to make the world a more beautiful place. Our phone conversations are pure delight!

My gratitude extends not only to Joel, but also to David for the life-changing experiences of the training. David continues to conduct public training and corporate consultations, along with Duanne. I quote him often. Learning to do self-examination with honesty is a wonderful thing.

In those days I met some amazing people and ate

some fabulous Tex-Mex food. These are some of the blessings of the journey.

Oh, and then there's Jeff—

The Lord works in strange and mysterious ways. It was my crush on this potential pastor that motivated my return to the church. The rest of the story reveals God's great sense of humor.

Jeff never went to seminary; rather, he found his calling among the laity.

Jeff and I never married, never even got close. *(Lord knows, I tried.)*

Jeff and I remain the best of friends. Our phone bills are much lower because of great cell phone plans. We talk regularly, and I count on him when I need a shoulder. We have shared life's highs and lows but never laundry. I love him.

So perhaps this would be a moment for you to take time and reflect. Who has been critical to your journey? To whom do you owe thanks for teaching and/or leading you to faith? Take some time to think of each of them and the unique roles they have played in your life. Thank them—out loud—or in writing. Raise them up in prayer. Thank God for them. Pray His blessings on them for their guidance on the road that led you home.

Good and Gracious God,
Creator of Love,

You reveal Yourself most fully in our relationships.
When we are close to others we are often able
to be closer to and better know You.
Help us to embrace one another with heavenly hugs.
Build gratitude in our hearts
and
Lead us home always to You.

Amen

7

How I Learned to be a Lutheran

For by grace you have been saved through faith,
And this is not from yourselves; it is the gift of God—
Not by works, so that no one can boast.

Ephesians 2:8-9

Grace is the free gift of God's love. Indeed!

Being a Lutheran, however, has a learning curve. And there is way more work to do than we might want to admit. There are proper liturgical responses (more on that later), when to stand (as you are able), and when to sit.

Yes—God has saved me. But His people taught me; sometimes directly, and on other occasions gently and swiftly. Discipleship took place even though I didn't always recognize it as such. Discipleship is the word I choose to describe what was happening then and continuing to the moment I write these words. It is the action of the Holy Spirit of God, working through people, which brings us ever forward in our faith journey. Growing in our own faithful walk must inevitably mean bringing others along with us.

My early days at Prince of Peace were overwhelmingly

emotional. I experienced worship in an entirely new way. My heart was opening to new possibilities. The Holy Spirit was at work so strongly that I didn't mind putting on pantyhose on Sunday morning in Arizona in June *(Two words: heat rash).*

Music lifted me, the proclamation/preaching of the Word stirred me, and the communion meal healed and restored me. I am not being overly dramatic here. Ask anyone who knew me then, and they will tell you that real transformation was occurring. I was falling in love. And yes—I was still very much attracted to Jeffrey, but my love was now aimed at Jesus, His church, and His people. I had spent so much of my life looking for love and suddenly (it seemed), there it was in front of me. In His life, death, and resurrection Jesus promised His committed love for me. Now I was responding. The love of my life was Jesus. *(Can I get an Amen!)*

I think it is true for most of us that, when in love, the possibilities for life seem infinite. I looked forward to Sunday morning and longed for some additional avenues to pursue this new relationship. Too new was I to volunteer, or so I told myself. I thought, when I was ready, I would. But, I didn't know how or where to start. Having been embraced by my new faith community, I was then drawn into the life of the parish. Servant opportunities were everywhere, but I just didn't know where to begin. Fortunately there were others ready to not only invite me in, but also walk with me.

Now—I'm gonna let you in on a little secret. This is something that I have learned over the last twenty-five-plus years in the church. If I knew then what I know now, what a difference there might be in my life today. My clergy friends wouldn't like me giving away trade secrets, but it will become obvious as I tell this story. So here goes:

The Sunday was rather ordinary. I don't recall much of the worship that day. What I do remember (vividly) was that my pantyhose were killing me. Now every woman has a pair that stays in the bottom of the drawer because they are just not right. They can't be thrown out because they have no runs or snags but they are the most uncomfortable pair you own. I considered them my emergency-only pair. *(If you can remember the days of pantyhose—you know exactly what I mean. If you cannot— thank your Lord!)*

As a consequence of the icky pantyhose, I was anxious to get away quickly following worship. I did the handshake with the pastor, moved quickly past the coffee fellowship, and sought a clear path to the parking lot. I knew I was at risk of excommunication for skipping coffee but it seemed to me a risk worth taking in order to get home and out of those damnable pantyhose.

On a beeline to my car, I thought I heard my name being called. Sure enough, as I stopped and turned around, there was Pastor Melissa halfway across the patio headed toward me.

I had enjoyed getting to know Melissa and was delighted that she pursued me. New to the church, I didn't realize what was about to happen. Here's one of the trade secrets of the clergy: if they follow you after worship, chances are good they will ask you to do something for which you would not have otherwise volunteered.

Sweet Melissa was smooth. She knew I was a newbie, and later told me she had been looking for the right place to draw me into the ministry of the parish. With her customary grace, she asked me to step into a support role for worship. Okay. I was intrigued. She continued. This role would be shared with two other women. Good, wouldn't have to do it alone.

The moment of truth came when Melissa spoke the words "co-chair of the Altar Guild." She had to inform me that the Altar Guild was the group who prepared the worship space and set the Communion table. It would be a great entry point for you, she said. She was so positive and assuring. She promised that plenty of people would be available to help me. My only consideration was that she had said "co-chair." How was I supposed to lead a group when I didn't really know what the group did?

Leadership was what she wanted from me. Based on my work experience, she felt I could "organize" this group into a cohesive unit. She seemed so confident. Melissa's faith in my ability to do this led to my own leap of faith. I said yes.

There were challenges in the beginning. The Altar Guild had become a less than cohesive group, and participation was down. These issues were addressed along with my co-chairs, Helen and Dorothy. Some of the longstanding *(translated: this is the way we have always done it)* procedures were changed. The parish moved from monthly communion to first and third Sundays.

Helen and Dorothy were patient, saintly women who taught me much about the nature of service in the church. My enthusiasm for the tasks at hand was properly grounded by a simple "Oh, really" from either one of them.

My favorite part was service in the sacristy. Our practice was to set the table elements on Saturday morning. It was on a Saturday morning that I received my initial training from an Altar Guild veteran named Evelyn. I am certain there is an Evelyn in every parish.

The Evelyns of our faith have built the church and kept it going. They are the women who do the work, often before being asked, because they know it must be done to keep the church rolling. Evelyns stand in worship without being told, because they know it is time. They teach us by their actions. Our churches would be far messier places without our Evelyns.

On this morning, Evelyn gave me a tour of the Sacristy. She showed me the beautiful custom paraments of the Prince of Peace Lutheran Church collection. These gorgeous linen altar appointments and pastoral vestments had been handmade with love by the Prince of Peace Christian Art Guild. Each had a story, and it was a joy to hear her tell them. She encouraged me to see the work at God's table as a privilege and honor.

Tour concluded, pep talk finished, it was time to get down to the business at hand. First, place a plastic cup in each hole of the tray. Easy enough. Now fill the cups in the outer ring with red wine. Not so easy. Mastering just the right squeeze to yield just the right amount of liquid to fill the cup without overfilling it took time. Evelyn was clearly anxious for me to get it (and stop making a mess), and she patiently encouraged me.

Next it was time for the wafers. I pointed to the covered brass and asked Evelyn if we used "these plates." She shuddered and responded, "Yes, those are the patens we use." Nomenclature has purpose. She pointed to the package of wafers for me to place on the patens. They came in a long tube. I took scissors to the wrappers and poured them onto the paten.

"Wait just a minute," Evelyn said. She continued with a question. "If you were having a party, would you just pour the crackers onto the plate?

"Of course not," I said. "I would probably make a cracker ring around the cheese ball or something pretty like that."

"I suppose so," Evelyn replied. She even told me she does something quite similar when she entertains guests in her home.

Then she asked, "Don't you think our Lord deserves that same care at His table?"

Ouch! She got me. In that brief exchange, she taught me so much about the real nature of the communion meal. I was there to set a table for the Lord to share with his friends. It should look pretty.

I picked up the wafers and made concentric rings on the paten. It was pretty! And I did indeed feel honored to place them on the altar for worship the following morning.

Besides an Evelyn, every parish should have a Ruth. The Ruth of that time in my life was a modestly dressed woman with a strong handshake and a bright smile. Ruth loved to greet people at or near the door. She took hold of your hand like she meant it. That warm handshake was accompanied by direct eye contact. She genuinely wished to connect to everyone. This was her ministry.

And she didn't just give you a faint "good morning." Hers was a far more personal, heartfelt message for each and every person. And it always ended with "May God bless your communion this morning." So much more powerful than a basic "good morning"!

Ruth was one of my great Lutheran teachers. One lesson came on my first Easter Sunday as a member of a Lutheran church. Lent had been a powerful time for me. It was an emotional time of reconnecting with Jesus. The Jesus I understood from my youth had given way to a new and more powerful understanding.

In those forty days of lessons, worship, and prayer, I quite simply fell in love with Jesus and His church. It's hard to explain the way I felt. It was an amazing time in my life. There is an intensity and intentionality of Lent. For forty days, I grew into my relationship with Jesus because I deliberately spent a significant amount of time reading, praying, worshipping, and serving. Doing all that and being a part of the community of faith, surrounded by others on their faith journeys, was important.

And I wanted to do it "right." I'm not exactly certain what that looked like. One thing I know is that the liturgy became a warm, safe place for me to allow the Holy Spirit to be at work in my life. What had first intimidated me was now part of what I loved about church. That spirituality could blossom within this context surprised me. It became the place where my faith journey was launched.

I also wanted to walk the path that others around me seemed to walk. I wanted the mature faith of some of the folks around me. Now, when I look back, I realize some of that was absolute folly. We must each take our own journey, walk our own path. Further, we must do it for ourselves, not for the sake of a misplaced sense of wanting to do it "right."

Holy Week had been particularly moving. The passion, which began so joyously on Palm Sunday, concluded with the immense pain and sorrow of Good Friday. Given all that, my desire for Easter morning was off the charts.

For the first time in my adult life, I had a grand time shopping for an Easter outfit. As a child I was always dressed well for Easter. But this time it was on me. I chose a baby-blue polka-dot dress with ruffled collar. It was fabulous! Remember, this was the 1980s.

Looking good and feeling good, I was delighted when I saw Ruth at her traditional spot at the front door. She was absolutely beaming. This day was special. Her greeting set the mood for the entire worship experience. Hand out, I stepped directly toward her.

Ruth took hold of my hand and said, "He is Risen!"

"Yes," I said.

With a slightly firmer hand and a somewhat puzzled look on her face, she repeated, "He is Risen!"

Still clueless, I said, "Yes, isn't it wonderful!" The reaction on her face let me know instantly that I had not done the Easter greeting properly. Heck, I didn't even know there was an "Easter Greeting."

Gracious Ruth somehow sensed that I was disappointed. Her hand took mine once again, this time quite gently. She stepped away from her greeter station and guided me around the corner to a private place. There in that corner she could teach me what she wanted me to know.

"Dear, this is how we do things on this day." So kind she was as she explained, "'He is Risen!' is responded with, 'He is Risen! Indeed!'" She went on to explain that we do it often during the Easter season, and usually repeat the call and response three times.

Again, taking me by the hand she led me back to the narthex. "We will start over," she declared. I was not willing to argue with this woman I adored.

Back at the front door, she held out her hand, looked me in the eyes, and said, "He is Risen!"

"He is Risen! Indeed!" was my reply. She hugged me and I knew that I had gotten it right.

Ruth's lesson to me that Easter morning really had little to do with what was "right." Her desire was for me to experience the beauty and power of the liturgy before the prelude began. Liturgy (meaning the work of the church) was Ruth's focus and passion. I wish every adult could have a Ruth in his or her life. Someone who always speaks truth and whose love and devotion to the Lord fosters your own.

Evelyn and Ruth were my more traditional Lutheran teachers. There were also a multitude of others who, in their way, taught me how to be a Lutheran.

Then there's Bob, the unconventional youth sponsor. We met one Sunday while I was working in the sacristy during communion. Bob was the "communion runner" responsible for bringing empty trays into us for refill. He came tripping in the door announcing: "They're a hungry bunch." I laughed out loud. That was only the first of many moments of laughter with Bob. He is funny and irreverent, faithful and sincere.

Bob taught me that the crucial rule in youth ministry was to "shirk responsibility." He said that kids can be responsible but won't be if you insist on being responsible for them. Sounds harsh, but it works when everybody understands the rules.

He had another rule: "If it's not fun, I'm not doing it." Some might say that's immature, and in another situation or another person that might be true. But with Bob that statement stood as an unequivocal pronouncement that joy could and would be found in all circumstances. And once joy was found, the fun was inevitable. Bob could make any activity wonderful.

I fear that naming some slights others. There are so many who have blessed me. Setting aside the risk of missing someone, I do want to share a few with you:

Teacher Kathy—Multiple generations of four-year-olds have been taught to love the Lord by this amazing lady. What a gift she is to the church. She and husband Ben have been surrogate grandparents to so many. Who knew their mixed marriage (he's Norwegian and she is Swedish) would last so long?

Friends Mary and Harry—Not long after joining the church and still taking baby steps on their faith journey, their second child was born prematurely. The community prayed for Greg's little brother Grant's survival. Grant did survive only to be diagnosed with two significant genetic anomalies that impacted both his physical and cognitive development. Rather than blame God or retreat from the church, Harry and Mary chose to lean into faith. They rolled up their sleeves to care for their sons and to continue to learn of God's grace. Miraculous is the only word appropriate to describe Grant's progress. Harry, Mary, Greg, and Grant continue to be an inspirational fulcrum to their congregation and to all who are blessed to know them. They are teachers in the way they live their lives and the way they love.

And there were clergy…

Pastor Melissa—The one who invited me into my first active role in the parish. Her gift is listening with compassion. She is equally gifted at laughing with you and crying with you. I understand the role of pastor from her.

Pastor Scott—This man is as close as I have to a brother. And he is Melissa's partner in marriage and ministry. Scott and I have worked on youth-related ministry for years. Among his gifts to me are understanding the Bible as a book of faith and clarity about God's calling to my life. He gave me my first professional speaking gig. We share an obsession for pens.

Pastor John—My former pastor and current friend. Later in this book you will read his role in my faith journey. John continually teaches me the beauty, power, simplicity, and truth of God's grace.

Jesus' Great Commission to *Go into all the world and preach the gospel…* (Mark 16:15) sometimes may seem a challenge beyond our reach. To respond feels outside our comfort zones. And, it might well be.

Yet Evelyn, Ruth, Bob, and the others were just as active in responding to Jesus' call as those who are doing important missionary work outside the country. They were making a disciple in their own neighborhood. Taking the time to teach a newcomer the ropes and remind one who continues are important to all on a journey of faith.

Those folks were God's hands and heart at work in my life. Living out their baptismal call, they shared themselves. They have and continue to bless me.

Oh, and while they may have taught me the Lutheran "stuff"—there was so much more. They taught me the value and blessing that is found in a Christ-centered life.

I pray we all have had great teachers, people who have influenced our lives for the better, whether or not they carry the professional title of "teacher." I have had great schoolteachers and great life teachers. For each of them I give thanks to God.

Take a moment to recall those folks. What did they teach you about life and/or about yourself? Have you ever told them of your gratitude and appreciation for what they have meant in your life?

Now—ask yourself this question: What do I teach? What does my life teach?

In some shape or manner we all have lessons to teach and gifts to share. What are yours? Avoid any tendency toward self-deprecation and answer yourself honestly. Take time to reflect. It will come to you. Pray for God-given clarity.

Then take your life and teach. Someone else's life may be waiting for the lesson you have to share.

Mine was.

Good and gracious God,
Risen Lord of life,

You call each of us into relationship
with You and Your entire creation.
Into each of us You have placed the ability
to be Your hands and heart to a world in need.
Give us strength and clarity
so that we may proclaim Your love with
joy and certainty.

We praise and thank You for our lives.

Amen

8

Hello, Paula—God Calling: A Big Story in Three Parts

"It was the best of times, it was the worst of times; …
it was the season of Light, it was the season of Darkness;
it was the spring of hope, it was the winter of despair;…"

—Charles Dickens

PART 1

My involvement in the church became very much the center of my life. The more I did, the more I wanted to do! Although there remained challenges and stress in my life, I had gained new perspectives on them. Much of the loneliness I had experienced was being replaced with new friends and fellowship.

The Altar Guild had provided a marvelous introduction to the church and left me wanting more. Before long I was elected to the church council and eventually worked in the areas of youth ministry, worship, and Christian education.

Clearly youth ministry had the most profound effect on me. And it began so quickly. Remember Bob, the youth worker whose sense of humor made me want to hang out, both with him and the kids? I told Bob of my interest in youth ministry—he spoke with Pastor Scott—and (yada yada yada)—I was a youth sponsor.

Joining the adult team, which supported youth ministry, in May made it necessary for me to get with the program quickly, the reason being, the high schoolers were preparing for their triennial trip to the ELCA National Youth Gathering in July. I needed to get ready to spend twenty-three hours on a bus traveling to San Antonio, Texas, with kids I had really just met.

Sometimes ignorance is a good thing. I had no idea the massive event I was about to experience. Remember I have been involved in a faith community for less than a year. Nothing could have prepared me for that first mass gathering of people. So much energy and love for the Lord.

And there were songs I had never heard before. And hand movements, which accompany the songs. The harder I tried the hand motions, the more I looked like someone trying to guide a plane up to a jetway. Ridiculous!

From that first trip, I knew that I loved hanging with young people. Their energy and enthusiasm for life is most attractive—attractive enough, in fact, to enable one to look past all those "squirrelly" teenage behaviors. Interactions with them were nearly as fun as the time spent with the adult sponsors. It takes a unique person to spend nearly every waking hour of their vacation time with teenagers; and by unique, I mean just a bit crazy. These folks were my earliest friends in the church. *(If I ever decide to write another book—*

I have enough stories from those youth ministry days to fill volumes.)

One really important thing happened in those early years of working with young people. My role (and that of other adult sponsors) was to engage them in conversations about life and faith. Discussions about life events can open the door to discussions of issues of faith. The critical element is to remain "real." Don't shy away when the interaction gets sticky and don't candy-coat the truth. Truth telling isn't easy, but it's always worthwhile.

I loved talking with those young people. They often asked tough questions. Never willing to take a simple answer, they pushed me to be honest with them. Sometimes that honesty was painful. Yet I treasured the opportunity those occasions provided, for they coaxed out of me a clarity about my faith, which was heretofore missing.

During one such time, I was sharing some of the tougher parts of "growing up gimpy." Relating the cruelty of school children to high schoolers who were not much older was tough. I respected them enough to be honest, and they expected nothing less.

One of the young men said to me, "God, Paula—and you didn't become a serial killer."

There was some nervous laughter around the group. He responded to the laughter, "No—seriously—I mean it." That was my cue that the question had to be answered. What was it that kept me from going off the deep end? What allows me to be joyful in the present with a past such as I had?

Here was my answer: "I believe it is a God thing." There was no one thing to which I could point to say "this" was *the* difference maker. I readily acknowledged the love and support of my parents. They had instilled in me strength of spirit, which proved of great value in facing life's challenges. Knowing of their love and support was essential.

Even the toughest in our group were hushed—a sure sign that they were processing what I said. I believe the Holy Spirit was stirring their interest in God through the hearing of my witness.

I continued. Sharing the power of a parent's love was important but it was essential for me to tell the whole story. Most important, I told them that God had shown me mercy and grace. Love without reservations, without any action on my part. I know clearly of my human limitations; I am no saint. And God loves me and forgives me. Once I understood that fact for myself, my perspective on others and their actions changed. Because if He loves and forgives me, that same love and forgiveness applies to others. Even to those who were cruel children.

My parents' love and support got me through in the moment. God's love enables me to speak of those incidents today. Further, it is God's great love and mercy that changes us all by forgiving even the worst of us. And, it allows us to move beyond the hurt that would otherwise hold us hostage.

Coming, as I did, from a long line of storytellers, it was natural for me to leap into the telling of God's story. I enjoyed it and found it personally rewarding. Whether an audience of one or many, I welcomed any opportunity to tell the story.

My life path was changing, and I hardly noticed. Clearly I knew that I loved life at work in God's church.

Besides youth ministry, I loved working in and around worship. When my parish formalized the role of a layperson as assisting minister, I was quick to volunteer to serve in the role. I loved it and felt completely at ease leading worship.

For a time, an interim pastor named Ruth served our parish. She was a wonderfully caring woman who led us through some pretty contentious days. I know it's hard to imagine that a congregation would be in turmoil,; but this particular parish had it down to an art form, and it seemed to be part of their DNA. *(Pastors come and pastors go, but a good argument can be recycled repeatedly.)*

All kidding aside, this parish has had its share of highs and lows. Ruth had come into our midst at a particularly low point. She won our hearts with her compassion for people and passion for the Lord. Wounds were given the time and space to heal, and the congregation regained a healthy footing. She was a blessing to our church.

She gave me a life-changing gift—one that proved eye opening. One day Ruth asked me into her office for a chat. She went straight to the point. "How would you like to preach a sermon?" She began on a strong note.

"A real sermon?" I asked.

She had a wonderful way of lightly laughing, which made my nervous meter settle down.

"Of course, a real sermon." Ruth proceeded to explain the opportunity she was offering. Our synod was meeting for Annual Assembly in Tucson, and she would be attending. The bishop had encouraged clergy to identify lay people within their congregations who could lead worship on Sunday (the final day of assembly). Ruth had chosen to offer this to me.

My reaction was a combination of "Oh, no" and

"Yes, please." It seemed a natural progression from being the assisting minister. And yet it was daunting.

"Do you think I can do it?" I asked. Silly question—she would not have asked unless she was confident I could do it. Really, I think I was just searching for affirmation.

After what I felt was sufficient balking—I didn't want to appear too eager and overly confident—I said, "Thank you—I'd love to do it." I could barely contain my enthusiasm. I was gonna get to preach! Oh my God—I was thrilled.

Ruth took lots of time to help me prepare. She gave me her copy of *Barclay's Commentary* for background information, then a brief overview of the law/gospel tension, which should be part of my reflection. Gratefully she never went into detail on the three-point sermon concept.

I left the meeting wondering if saying yes was the right thing to have done. It was so much more complicated than I could ever have guessed. What was I thinking?

Fortunately I had a little over a month to get it together. Ruth's door was open and she promised whatever help I needed. My friends were excited for me and said they would all be there. Oh great—no pressure!

In those days, I worked for a small regional hospital in Cottonwood, Arizona, about two hours north of Scottsdale. The job was great, but the small town was no place for a single woman. So my week was there, and weekends were spent at home in Scottsdale.

Evenings were a great time for preparation and study. The more I read the *Barclay's Commentary*, the more I wanted to read. I must have read the scripture text in five or six translations. My thirst for the work was surprising and motivating. All of it was so new to me, and I was really enjoying the process. I was even so excited that I told my boss, Reid Wood, the hospital CEO. He was an articulate and witty man with a vocabulary the likes of which I hadn't heard since my father. He appeared out of place in that small town. He could be frustrating to work for, but he was always quite supportive of me. We enjoyed talking and even debating religion. Debate we did, because Reid was a member of the Church of Jesus Christ of Latter Day Saints. He was a Mormon.

Before I left on Friday afternoon, Reid asked me to record my sermon so that he could hear it the following week. I took that as a compliment.

My sermon had gone from full written script to key phrases on a series of notecards. Ruth had offered her alb for me to wear. I felt ready; everything seemed to be coming together.

As nighttime devotion on Saturday, I read again the text for the next day's sermon. It was from John 17; Jesus prays His high priestly prayer in the Garden of Gethsemane. It is beautifully poetic and powerful when understood in the context of the events that immediately follow. In that time of reading and reflection, the challenge I was about to undertake was nearly overwhelming.

Sunday morning came and brought with it the peace that passes understanding. I was at ease in my skin and confident that, by the grace of God, all would be well.

In the vestry I had tears when I saw myself in the mirror. Dressed in the alb seemed different this morning. I had worn a white robe to serve communion when

I was assisting minister, but this was so much more. Looking into the mirror, I felt as though I was seeing my true self. My identity was becoming clearer to me. Was this the point to which all my other work in the church was leading? I could not be certain except for one thing: I liked what I saw and how I felt.

The service went well and my sermon was well received. Granted, I had packed the audience with family and friends. Words of affirmation from worshipers filled my heart with delight.

When all was over, I sat in the sanctuary alone. Emotionally and physically, I was exhausted. Spiritually, however, I was in a place of peace and open to the Spirit's leading. My prayers were of gratitude to God for the opportunity to serve and glorify Him in this manner. For once in my life, I did not attempt to analyze my thoughts and feelings. Just letting them be is not my style, as I always want to understand what I'm feeling and what it all means. That day I simply sat in the beauty of the sanctuary and communed with my Lord.

I returned to my job in Cottonwood on Monday, taking with me the cassette (*yes—it was that long ago*) for my boss. As I left it with his secretary, I was a little anxious to hear his review. He would be honest and so I best prepare myself.

The following afternoon, Reid called me into his office. This would be the time for his review. Why did I want his approval? Beyond the fact that he was my boss and it is always good to impress the boss, he was a well-read, articulate, and faithful man. I admired his intellect.

"Great delivery, lousy theology," was his succinct review.

I laughed out loud. It was probably a good thing that our theology did not match. Perhaps the nicest thing he could say was to compliment my delivery. He was an accomplished orator and I took his praise with high regard and gratitude.

Over the years that I worked for him, he would occasionally call me to his office during the late afternoon. He simply wanted to chat. It helped him clear his mind he said. Sometimes we even debated our religious differences. It was an exercise we both enjoyed and some of my favorite memories of the time I spent there.

More opportunities to preach came my way over the coming years. Those times and all the rest of my time serving and working in the church began to pull at my heart. The Holy Spirit was doing what the Spirit does best—remind us of God's desire for us to live fully into the gifts we have been given. On more than one occasion, I had people ask me if I was interested in the ordained ministry. Pastor Scott had started that so many years earlier, and now the chorus of voices was growing. I began to believe there was merit to the idea.

For two more years I wrestled with the whole notion of going to seminary and pursuing the ordained ministry. My sense of call was being reinforced by the work I did with youth as well as adult Bible study and assisting in worship.

I did not have an epiphany moment in the sense of a singular bolt of light. Rather, I began to feel haunted by the Holy Spirit. There was more of a constant pulling at my soul, which, although I tried to ignore it, I could not shake. God was not to be ignored. I was being drawn to a place that was both frightening and exciting. God had taken hold of my heart, and it was time for me to listen.

There were many considerations to be addressed. We Lutherans have no seminaries in warm, dry climates. They are located in places where it is either cold, damp, or on the side of a hill. None of them would work for this gimpy gal.

Fifteen years ago, the church did not have much in the way of alternate routes to ordination that would work for me. My frustration grew each time I hit a dead end. I believed God was calling me, but that the church organization wasn't ready for me.

My friend and pastor John Cockram was so very supportive and willing to mentor and support me in any way possible. He introduced me to seminary faculty when they were in town. Always, we carried into those meetings the hope that someone would have an answer. John also advised me that I needed to have faith that the church will, one day, respond. I understood the need for patience. Like it or not, we are working on the timetable of someone else.

And then there is God's time…

Pastor John called and told me that we would be having dinner with the president of Wartburg Seminary. John was a Wartburg graduate and knew the president. The seminary presidents were in town for their annual gathering, and John had arranged for us to meet with Dr. Roger Field.

With great anticipation I spent most of the day trying to figure out what I would wear. *(I guess that's a girl thing.)* But this would be a different kind of meeting, the closest we had gotten to a "decision maker." This man had the ability to make allowances that would make seminary education possible.

My anxiety was quickly calmed by this genuinely thoughtful, kind, godly man. Both Roger and John were men with a love for Jesus and his church. Consequently, once all the facts were shared, they quickly moved into brainstorming creative options for my seminary education. I sat in wonder.

Initially, I was saddened as they both acknowledged the church's lack of a comprehensive alternative route to ordination. That time had not yet come. Yet before I could invite anyone else to my pity party, they came up with an ingenious idea.

The layout at Wartburg seminary makes it possible for students to live, attend class, study, and eat without leaving the building. If I were willing to stay inside during the most inclement weather, Wartburg would work for me. Roger was even willing to consider an air-conditioning unit for my room. He said it would make me popular on campus to have a cooled room. How delightful. That actually seemed a wonderful compromise to me.

PART 2

"We would love to have you at Wartburg Seminary." My mind stumbled to absorb the words my ears, I prayed, were actually hearing. Did I just hear the president of the seminary welcome me into the next phase of my faith journey?

We ended our conversation with some of the details that needed to be addressed. There are always details, aren't there? We in the church are big on details. I must say, I find something comical about how we Lutherans preach "Grace Alone" and yet are obsessed with details of our own creating. Oh well!

One of those details would be a psychological assessment. Would I be emotionally fit for the challenge of seminary and then ordained ministry? I fully recognize the value of a psychological assessment. I have worked with too many people (outside of the church and a few inside) who appeared to me emotionally ill prepared for the jobs they were holding. And yet this, as well, seems a bit comical to me; but if we truly embrace the fact that the Holy Spirit of God calls us into the ministry, do we not believe that God calls those who are capable? (*Oh Lord—I'm getting lost in the intellectual weeds again.*)

One of my personal details to be addressed: I had a job. It was a good job, working as the vice president for a small but vibrant regional hospital. Having taken the job because it was the best option at the time, I found wonderful people and professional satisfaction working in this place. And, as I have told you earlier, I really enjoyed my boss, Reid Wood. It was, therefore, with no small amount of trepidation that I walked into Reid's office that day to request a leave of absence.

After years of praying and wrestling with the Holy Spirit of God, my mind was made up. The invitation from the seminary had removed the last obstacle. Knowing the personnel policies (it helped that I had written them), I decided to request a two-year educational leave of absence. Although it would not guarantee my job, a leave of absence would provide some extension of benefits. As well, the two-year timeframe coincided with the church's candidacy process. This would be two years of learning and discerning the true nature of my call.

Looking back now, I wonder if I was somehow hedging my bet—trying, it might appear, to keep one foot in a world I knew, while gingerly placing one foot on the path to a new calling. After all, I did love my work in the hospital, and perhaps that was where I was supposed to be. Time and the Spirit would tell.

Reid had known of my active faith and my wrestling heart from our regular conversations about faith, life, and the nature of the divine. Well read and devout, he was an excellent conversationalist, particularly on such matters. And although our theology differed, we had enjoyed wonderfully open communication. Ours, you see, was a strange and wonderful relationship.

Secure as I felt in that relationship, I was still about to ask for a leave. Set aside the fact that I was about to ask for leave to pursue ordained ministry from a man whose religion did not accept the ordination of women. Complicating the situation, my leave was coming at a potentially hectic stage in the business life of the hospital where rumors of merger filled the air.

"Mr. Wood, I have a request."

"No," he said. I had learned early in my tenure that "no" was always his first response. I surmise that it had something to do with having so many children.

Despite his initial denial, it took only a little begging. We each did our share. I carefully outlined my reasons.

He graciously implored me to reconsider and stay. He then acknowledged the inevitable and approved my leave of absence. I nearly gushed with excitement.

On my last day, there was a reception with cordial goodbyes from members of the board of directors, hospital staff, and friends. Reid's final words to me were on the cake. It was a quote from one of his favorite movies: Come Back Shane.

The only thing left before heading to Iowa was a little "body and fender" work. This is my term for the upkeep that is required for a body, which, like mine, is held together with glue and bolts.

Bodies are at once both beautiful and bedeviling. Physicians have created ways to fix problems. As I have shared earlier, I have been the beneficiary of many advances in medicine. My body is a testament to the power of innovation to improve lives. These fixes, however, are not always permanent and consequently require maintenance.

The body parts in greatest need of attention at that time were my elbow implants. Both needed to be replaced. The plan would be to do the left elbow first, heal, and then do the right. No problem—I had been down this road before. Seminary may be a new chapter with uncharted water, but surgery was something I knew.

Mother and I (along with Aunt Carol) headed to the hospital that morning just as we had on so many other occasions. The hospital team, the trio of long standing, we have been there and done that so many times. Anxiety was, as always, a part of my pre-op morning. It doesn't get any easier with experience. But there was a difference that particular morning. Mitigating my usual angst was my confidence that this was a step toward my goal—my dream of seminary. Each time my nerves cranked up, I tried to visualize myself on the day of ordination.

Awaking in the PACU (Post Anesthesia Care Unit—known to most as the recovery room) after surgery is best described as surreal. The experience includes thinking you are awake, yet not being completely certain you are; and trying to speak, yet not hearing any sound. Add to those feelings tremendous pain, and you get the picture.

It was in the PACU that I first thought I had a problem. I asked for a washcloth in order to "cock-up" my wrist as I felt it dangling and unsupported. By the time I was transferred to my regular room, there was an obvious problem. My left hand was swollen and numb. Swollen and numb is never a good combination, particularly after surgery. Additionally, it was painful and worse yet, dysfunctional. It wouldn't move.

My God—I wondered and prayed—what was wrong with me? When will it be right? My running monologue with the Great Physician ran something like this: I gotta have my left hand, Lord…you know that it is the one that does all the work…remember Lord…I didn't complain when the arthritis made my right wrist stiff…I took it in stride…well, that's because I had ol' lefty to rely on…come on, Jesus…help me.

As the symptoms persisted, my nervous meter went straight through the roof. We had hoped that the dysfunction was a result of some sort of surgical trauma (the tourniquet was the likely culprit), which would, with time, abate. Function would then return. So why not hope? Hope is a good thing! Hope had been my trademark. Hope, and my ability to cling to it, had, I believed, been a special gift from God to me.

Besides hope, I had trust. Trust in a wonderful physician whose compassion and expertise had allowed me so many chances to live a normal life. He had operated when others might not. Lord knows my life wouldn't have been as independent had I not met, and been in the care of, this very special doctor. I trusted him. For all he had done for me, he deserved my trust and confidence.

Having said all that, I still could not shake my anxiety about the dysfunction, which persisted in my hand. Nobody could answer my simple questions: What is wrong with me? Why? Is it going to resolve on its own—or will further surgery be required? Questions lead to more questions like: What kind of surgery? Who would do the procedure? And then the big one—When?

We humans do not deal well when our questions have no answers. And not only were there no answers, I had no sense of where else to go to find any answers. I was stuck at one very long red light on the road of life. Looking forward, it was as though there were no roads. Helplessness overcame me. Not the kind of helplessness from an inability to do something for myself like tie my shoes; this was the kind that comes from feeling unable to choose a new path. I was stuck and could not move in any direction.

This was in direct contradiction to the way I was raised to live my life. This was in total opposition to the strength of my ability to face the situation. Handle it and keep moving. That has always been my way. I am

Paula, a strong and lovable woman, a sinner of God's own redeeming. I have been in the company of adversity my whole life, and I'm still standing. This should not be slowing me down, let alone stopping me cold.

Lying in bed each night, I promised myself renewed energy and enthusiasm for overcoming the obstacles before me. My psych-up was really half prayer and half pep talk. And through the collision of prayer and pain medication, I drifted off into sleep certain that tomorrow would be a better day. It was wonderful.

Morning arrived and I remember cherishing the moments of awakening, still full of hope for all the day held. And then, like most people, I arose and headed to the bathroom where my optimism would quickly end. Reality—damn reality—hit me. There in my bathroom, where no one else could see, the tears began again. My hand would not reach where I needed, or effectively hold the toilet tissue. I was thirty-eight years old and forced to call my mother to help me clean up after toileting. (Now you may ask yourself, why doesn't she use her other hand? Well, my right hand and arm just plain do not reach. My elbow bends very little—about fifteen degrees and I can only wipe the back with my left hand. (Too much sharing?)

My great mental talent for compartmentalization (meaning that which was not of immediate importance could be set aside) became a two-edged sword. I could go through my day, finding ways to work around problems with the arm, only to run into a brick wall in those activities that were just plain impossible. Simple things, like eating a submarine sandwich or a good hamburger loaded with toppings, hit the impossible list. Anything that required two hands was difficult, if not impossible.

I find words hard to come by when remembering those days. My broken spirit now equaled the harsh reality of my broken body. My memory is mostly of the impossibly steep hill that was before me. And there was no clear path up, over, or around the hill.

As I write these words, it is fifteen years later. Even I am shocked at the realization of the time that has passed. Out of all the difficulties and seemingly insurmountable challenges, there continues to be life.

How did this happen? Small accomplishments—one day at a time.

Medically, things started to resolve when we finally determined what had happened. It took three different doctors, an MRI, and multiple EMGs (a test for muscle/nerve function), all of which I preferred not to endure again. The diagnosis was not what I wanted to hear. The radial nerve in my left arm had been severed during the surgery. My original surgeon (the man I had trusted) was actually the one who figured out the story. Here is my laywoman's description: Picture a small drill used to clean out the inside of a small stick. In my case it was a surgical drill cleaning residual glue out of the inside of my humerus. Turns out that my humeral bone was thin and, without realizing it, the doctor's drill had gone through the bone from the inside to the outside and cut the nerve lying alongside the bone. It was a "blind injury."

With no radial nerve, the function of my hand was significantly impaired. This is the nerve that innervates the hand to flex and to release grip. Now we understood why my hand lay flaccid at the end of my arm, and, without support, bent down, and my thumb curled under.

It is beyond weird to look down at a hand and fingers that will not move. The rest of me was working, but not this. My empathy for paralyzed people shot through the roof. I am convinced that special strength comes to those who must deal with the loss of mobility. People in such circumstances are in my prayers regularly.

Hope began to shine again when my old friend and gifted hand surgeon, Dr. Leonard Bodell, joined my team. My affection for him personally was exceeded only by the trust I had for him professionally. Lenny spoke in plain language without sugar coating the hard stuff. He presented a two-pronged approach. First, he would perform a tendon transfer to allow me a modicum of control over my hand. And, secondarily, he thought it worth the effort to attempt to reconnect the nerve. Others had told me that such reconnection was possible. In his hands, I was willing to give it a whirl.

Long story short: the tendon transfer has been a great success, but the nerve reconnection did not work. As it turns out, the nerve was like an old rubber band, frayed on each end. It was so very worth the effort, and I am grateful for the hope it brought me. Like I have said many times, I can live with pain, and I can live with this level of function, but I cannot live without hope.

My "call" to ordained ministry was now on hold. The opportunity at Wartburg was hard to decline, but it was necessary to do so. The challenges of going to school were complicated by my inability to live independently. With the tendon transfer, I was able to re-learn how to handle toileting independently. Yet, the dysfunction in my hand made every task either more complicated, or exhausting, or both. The resources to hire personal aides were just not available. I would not be moving to Iowa.

Returning to work at the hospital was also out of the question. Bathing and dressing were difficult and took a considerable amount of time. I was no longer able to use a keyboard, as this was long before quality voice-activated software. And the hours of an executive were nearly impossible, as my overall health had degenerated as well.

My educational leave of absence was converted into an application for long-term disability. I applied and was approved for Social Security Disability on my first attempt. People who have been through this process, either for themselves or for a loved one, know that such approvals rarely come quickly. Mine did. At this point, that seemed the only bit of silver lining in the dark cloud that hung over me.

Once beyond the shock of the physical, I dealt with the emotional reality of lost dreams. Truthfully, I spent some time being quite angry with God. After all, I had left a good job and committed myself to His service, and here I was. WHY ME? What a worthless question! Yet, I asked it with passion. No matter the passion or frequency with which I asked, the question is empirically fruitless. The answer changes nothing!

The only answer to "Why me?" is "Why not me?" Lord only knows.

PART 3

I did the only thing I knew to do. I went back to church. Hearing God's Word in the company of the saints is the most marvelous balm for a wounded spirit. In preparation for moving to Iowa, I had ended all my commitments within the parish and so was left with only worship. It was a good thing.

As the summer came to a close, Pastor John and his wife Tonya returned from their time away with a renewed and revitalized vision for the confirmation program at Prince of Peace Lutheran Church. New curriculum had been written and would be implemented using adult mentors from the congregation working in small groups with the students. When Pastor John and Tonya are excited about something, it is difficult not to be excited along with them. This was no different. Mentor groups and the opportunity to work one on one with the students intrigued me.

I knew their new confirmation program would be of value, great value, in our parish. But my experience and ministry had always been with high school–aged folks. Personally, I had no interest in spending time with children in the sixth grade. Sixth through eighth grades had been very difficult for me. I held many hurts from those days—hurts that made me resistant to spending time around kids that age. So I was delighted for Pastor John and Tonya, but not at all interested for myself.

Recall from a previous chapter where I shared that clergy have unique ways of inviting you to do something for which you would not otherwise volunteer. This talent also extends to clergy spouses. Tonya's technique is to casually sit down next to you in the fellowship hall with a cup of coffee in hand. Small talk ensues, and before you know it she has you engaged in conversation about her latest project or plan. And you are so engaged that you don't even realize you're being set up for the big question.

On this particular day, Tonya and I sat over coffee and she shared with me the new confirmation program.

She spoke of how exciting it would be for young people to form relationships with adults and that, in so doing, their faith would be encouraged. Gone would be the days of pastor lecturing to the children. They would be replaced by small group discussions with Pastor and adult mentors. Everything she said resounded in my heart. It all sounded so exciting. Then came the big question.

Tonya invited me to be one of the adult mentors. And although I was excited about her new program, I still had my concerns about my own ability to work with children of this age. I asked her forbearance, as I needed to spend time in prayer. This, of course, was no problem. I suspect Tonya already knew, somehow, what my answer would be.

In my prayers over the next couple of days, God and I wrestled with being intrigued and fearful in the same moment. I wanted so badly to be a part of this new program, and yet my fears from my past were standing in my way. Damn fear! Fear cripples us in ways that disease cannot. Fear holds us back and limits our vision. Fear breeds in the darkness of our uncertainties. And fear can only be defeated when our focus is on the light. Jesus is the light of the world and in him there is certainty. Fear is vanquished.

I knew better than to be afraid. But knowing better is only of value when it leads us to doing better. If you want to be unafraid, then act unafraid. Or fake it till you make it.

One other thing I have failed to mention thus far. It is nearly impossible to say "no" to Tonya. She has a marvelous gift for matching people and task, and then ensuring that you have the support necessary to feel successful. I must admit I knew that I couldn't say no to Tonya. If Jesus could move me beyond my fears, then Tonya would fit my skills to the challenge.

I did have one additional consideration, a quite selfish one. I had loved the work I did with high school–aged folks. I appreciated the conversations we had about issues of faith as they intersected our lives. Teenagers get a bad rap for only being able to think at a surface level. I would miss being involved in their lives.

Truthfully, I also thought that junior high–aged folks were more immature than I was prepared to handle. Would I be able to have meaningful conversations with them? I wondered. I doubted. If there were to be decent productive relationships with them, I would need an attitude adjustment.

Our confirmation classes met on Sunday afternoons. The curriculum was arranged in a way that allowed students to complete workbook-style packets with the assistance of adult mentors in small groups. Once each packet was completed, students met in small groups with one of the pastors for review. Each packet and concluding review included memory verses. All of the requirements for completion of confirmation (packets, review, and memorization) were displayed on a chart in our classroom. At the beginning of a two-year confirmation process, the task seems enormous. This led to a considerable amount of grumbling from students and occasionally even from their parents.

Into this environment came a small group, of which I was a member, who would act as adult mentors for these confirmation students. Our job was to help them learn. In order to help them learn, we had to get past their resistance and anxiety about the program. Our process for confirming young people included retreat weekends. This was about the only part of the program that excited them. It was the expectation that the adult mentors would participate in retreat weekends. For me, this was the only part of the program that did not excite me. *Two years*, I kept telling myself, *two years*.

Preteen behavior is an odd mix of craziness and crankiness, sweetness and sneakiness, and a full measure of "expect the unexpected." It was a challenge for me in the beginning. I did not care for these kids who could hardly sit still. They acted like four-year-olds. Their behavior brought out some of my less-attractive qualities.

But they got to me. I don't mean in a negative way. Somewhere along the line, they snuck into my heart. Each and every time I found myself getting frustrated by their wacky behavior, I took it as a challenge to find yet another way to tell the story. Perhaps they would understand better if I taught better.

Language was a critical part of this plan. I needed them to know that God's story, although told with sometimes ancient phrasing, is still relevant. We laughingly called it the NPT—New Paula Translation. I set out to make the Word meaningful, and so I needed to begin with making it understandable. This was true for the people in the Bible. My group needed to know that Saul of Tarsus was a bounty hunter before God came calling. They understood bounty hunter better than "Saul carried letters to secure."

One afternoon, some from my group were ready for their review with the pastor. A boy named Wiley had been one of my special cases. The harder he resisted learning, the harder I tried to teach him. Finding ways to get through to him became one of my goals. He had completed the packet about the apostle Paul and was now ready for his review, along with others, at the table with Pastor John. Pastor John would engage them in conversation about what they had learned and in so doing he would know whether they really had learned anything or had simply filled in the blanks on their sheets.

Pastor John opened the review by turning to Wiley and saying, "Tell me something about Saul of Tarsus."

Wiley's response was classic. He said, "Well, Pastor John, that guy was one bad-ass dude." I heard it with my own ears and held my breath, waiting for Pastor John's reaction.

"Were you in Paula's group?" was Pastor's first question. He already knew the answer.

I sheepishly looked toward Pastor John and the table where the review was being held and simply smiled. The kid had gotten the answer right. Pastor John knew it. I knew it. And most importantly, Wiley knew it. Their review continued and the students went on to answer Pastor John's questions and get their gold star for completing their packet.

Pastor John came to me at the end of class that day and said, "I appreciate what you're trying to do, but, the language?!" "Whatever works," was my answer.

And as for memorization—the ultimate bribe was needed. Candy and french fries worked as perfect motivators for learning those scripture verses and parts of Luther's Small Catechism. Every kid loves an old lady with a bag full of chocolates.

And yes, there were retreat weekends. My trepidation about them had more to do with my creature comforts than the actual amount of time spent with young people. But we had a good camp and always had fun when on retreat. There were always marvelous opportunities to get to know the young people on a different level. I taught some of them how to play poker—guess that pretty much ruins my chances in a Baptist church—and others how to string beads and make jewelry. The activities were far less important than the time it allowed us to spend with the kids.

And just like I had shared so many years earlier with high school–aged folks, I found opportunities to share with these young people my junior high struggles. More of them struggle with social and relationship issues than we can possibly imagine. When I told them of my own struggles, we suddenly had ground that we shared. They would ask me how I survived, and I would comfortably reply "only by the grace of God."

Both in classrooms and on retreats there were opportunities to minister with both the young people and my fellow adult mentors. I became comfortable with public prayer. Consequently, I was able to pray with and for the group as readily as I was able to pray for myself. I found ease within my own skin. I had found a peace, the kind of peace that can only come from Jesus.

My life had meaning and purpose once again. This was not the ministry to which I had previously felt called, but it was the ministry God had given me. I adopted the position that, inasmuch as God has never said no to me, I will do my best to never say no to Him.

Our first students in that confirmation program were sixth graders. The program normally ran from seventh through eighth grades, but because of the demographics of the congregation it was important for us to begin with sixth graders this one time. This meant that these young people were confirmed in the eighth grade. This notch group faced one additional challenge. For fellowship and socialization, they were neither high school nor confirmation group eligible.

My heart broke for these young people particularly when we came to understand that they would be excluded from the ELCA national youth gathering because they were underage. Our high school group would be focusing on preparations for attending the gathering. There would be very little of value for that group in participating in our high school Luther league.

I volunteered to create a one-year group for these kids. We would have our own Sunday school class and we would prepare to take a trip of our own. Remember, these kids had worked their way into my heart and I was not willing to let go of them. They were **my** kids now.

We had a wonderful year together. Some Sundays we had open discussion, and on others we had more formal curriculum. We made plans and preparations for a trip at the end of our school year. Fundraising and group-building activities were done. I was so very grateful for the support of Pastor John and these kids' parents.

We decided to take a weekend trip. My only rule had been that the trip must include time for both fun and mission work. It was finally determined that we would begin by heading to San Diego, California, where we would spend our first night. The next day included a trip to SeaWorld and the beach. Saturday night we would drive to Yuma, Arizona. Sunday morning we would meet with a pastor who would guide us into San Luis in Sonora, Mexico. We would visit an orphanage there, bringing gifts of food and clothing. At the end of the day we would drive home to Phoenix.

It was a whole lot of trip to pack into a short amount of time. But our financial resources were limited, and I was concerned for the maturity of these young people on a long trip. I was, however, not willing to settle for a simple play trip. We needed to be about the work of Jesus if this trip was to have any lasting value in the lives of these young people.

I had wonderful adult sponsors, including Pastor John, Gary (one of the parents), and sisters Julie and Lori (high school sponsors) who would handle the physical rigors of the trip. Our kids came from differing socio-economic backgrounds, yet they were all friends who got along well and, for the most part, behaved themselves.

The first leg of the trip went smoothly. SeaWorld and the beach are places that make us all smile. The cool weather in San Diego was a welcome break from the heat of Phoenix. By Saturday evening, everyone had his or her fill of sand and surf. The two-hour drive to Yuma gave them time to sleep. This was a good thing because the following day would challenge us all.

Sunday morning, before leaving our motel, we filled our coolers with ice and soda pop, which we planned to share with the children at the orphanage. We met our guide and began the trek into San Luis, Sonora, Mexico. The distance was short but it seemed a world away.

The reality of the poverty in this Mexican border town was overwhelming to our young people and frankly to the adults as well. Our children had led relatively privileged lives and had never seen poverty in such an up-close and personal fashion. We wound our way through dirt streets to what appeared to be a building without windows. In reality, the walls were the enclosure around the orphanage. Once our guide made contact with the headmistress of the orphanage, the iron gates were opened and we were allowed in.

All of us grew silent. We did not know what to say. I think we were simply overwhelmed. This orphanage was home to some thirty children ranging in age from babies to thirteen- or fourteen-year-olds. The older children were all girls. We were told this is because boys are expected to earn their own living once they reach twelve. The older girls help the staff of two care for the rest of the children.

The children of the orphanage were gathered into one room (one of the two with concrete floors) in order to meet us. We spoke very little Spanish, and they spoke almost no English. We were grateful for our guide and his ability to do our translations. We learned how to tell our names and how to say hello. I wish we had spent our time preparing for the trip by learning a little more Spanish.

Language proved to be unnecessary when we carried in our coolers full of soda pop. We also brought licorice, cookies, and all sorts of other goodies. Our kids connected with those kids over cans of root beer. Before long they were playing games out on the makeshift playground. Pastor John was even giving "horsey rides" on his knees to the littlest ones. Gary was a big man back then, and I think the children rather thought he was Santa Claus because all they wanted to do was sit on his lap. He obliged them.

Each of our kids seemed to form an attachment to

one or two of the orphans. A couple of our boys had worn their fancy sunglasses, yet I saw them more often on the faces of two or three of the orphaned children. Girls were braiding little girls' hair and sharing headbands. The children from the orphanage were being held and played with more than they had in a long time. It's just not possible in a setting with so few adults.

We unloaded the remainder of our offering and took as many pictures as we could before loading up in our vans for the long drive home. As difficult as it had been to get our group out of the vans when we first arrived, it was now nearly impossible to get them loaded back in to go home.

As we began to drive out of the compound, the children and adults of the orphanage were lined up waving goodbye to us. As I looked into my rearview mirror I saw another touching sight. My kids were on their knees, looking backwards in order to keep contact with those little children as long as possible. The ride from Mexico back into Yuma (where we would drop off our guide) was nearly silent.

We brought our trip to a close at a site that is traditional for Luther League trips: the Dairy Queen. Everyone went into the Dairy Queen for an ice cream and a little discussion. Pastor John asked them a simple question: "We have packed a lot into this weekend. What was your favorite part?" Normally there is a pause as they wait to see who will go first. Not that day. Each one of them was anxious to tell us how much they enjoyed their trip to the orphanage. Each and every one said that they would remember it always and hoped to return there again.

I tell you that story to conclude this chapter because it was the moment in which my life regained a clearer sense of purpose and value. So many things had gone wrong in my life and in my body, yet this had gone so right that all that came before seemed to pale in comparison.

God's work was being done. Young people were learning the lessons of grace and giving. And I had found in those children something I had never had. I had always wanted to be a mother. It's perhaps the great disappointment of my life. These kids had filled that empty spot in my heart.

Those young people are adults now, many with children of their own. I have been privileged to remain a part of many of their lives. I feel a connection to every child that has ever been in one of my groups. I have performed the marriage ceremony for some of them and even baptized a couple of their children. I love all of them—almost like a mom.

God has gifted and called each of us. He laid His claim on us at our baptism and never backed away. Whether we fully recognize it or not we each have a God-given purpose. We may, in fact, spend an inordinate amount of time running from our true calling. Sometimes we cite humility (which is often mis-identified) as the reason for stepping away from our Godly calling. On other occasions we may beg inadequacy. We say that we don't know "how." For whatever reason, claiming our giftedness is a challenge. Yet it is a challenge most worth pursuing.

What are your God-given gifts, talents, and passions? Do you ever take the time to recognize what God has already done in your life? Remember that God promised His people (through Abraham and Sarah) they were "blessed to be a blessing."

May I suggest that you take the time to journal. Write down, somewhere, anywhere, how you have been blessed. Be concrete. Blessings are often things that you can see, feel, touch, and/or hold. Then be a little less concrete in your thinking and consider your intangible blessings.

Now it gets a bit tougher. Answer these questions: How are you blessing others? How do you take those tangible and intangible blessings and use them to bless others?

Lastly—the kicker—do you do the blessings in the name of the One who blessed you? Do people know you are responding to God's gracious blessing—and not just being "nice"?

Good and gracious God,
Lord of my heart,

For the many ways in which You have taken hold of my life
and the times which You have loved me
beyond my own understanding,
let my life and heart be forever in Your safe-keeping.
In each day and in every way,
let my life be a glorious reflection
of your love—not only for me—
for the entire world.
Compel me and enable me
to respond to the gifts You have given to me.

Amen

9

Becoming Miss Paula

"I will be glad and rejoice in you;
I will sing the praises of your name, O Most High."

—Psalm 9: 2

In the fall of 1997, our associate pastor accepted the call to develop a mission congregation in north Scottsdale. The congregation (Prince of Peace Lutheran Church) took the news hard, as Pastor Tim had been a much-loved part of the ministry team. Among his primary responsibilities had been our high school youth program. He had recruited a group of quite capable lay volunteers, but his exit was hard for the young people and their parents. I was by then focused on the confirmation program, but the high schoolers who were missing him had been my confirmation kids years before. My heart ached for them as they grieved.

Pastor Tim's departure left holes in staffing the ministry at Prince of Peace. The call process for a second pastor began, but there would be some time before a new person would be in place. Volunteers could and did pick up some of the work, but there were a cadre of things that were difficult to cover with volunteer help alone. This is a dilemma churches face with some regularity. There are risks associated with these kinds of staffing challenges, and they run the gamut from reduced ministry activity or support to serious burnout of the staff that remain in place.

My working background in human resources and organizational development made me acutely aware of the possible problems. My friend and then senior pastor, John Cockram, had his hands full. The ministry of the parish was vibrant. A highly successful preschool, thriving Sunday school including both children and adults, youth ministry programs, and all the other "stuff" of a church meant that Pastor John would need help. Asking for help is not something I do well; so it is without judgment that I say I doubted he would.

I was shocked when, following worship one Sunday morning, Pastor John approached me with an uncharacteristically bold comment. "We, my friend, need to talk."

My first instinct was to think I had done something wrong. I don't know why that happens. Somehow, I instantly return to being fifteen years old, when I had more than likely done something wrong, and my mother wanted to "talk." Consciousness of guilt, I suppose. I managed to get a grip on myself and said I'd meet him in his office momentarily.

Pastor John got right to the point. "I need help, and I think you're just the person I need." This was my friend and mentor asking for my help. I was stunned. Stunned that he asked for help and equally so that he asked that help from me. I was also elated; elated that he would express his need, and more so that he believed me capable.

John laid out his hope that I would commit some

specific time to the church and partner with him in a sort of administrative coordinator role to support all of the ministries of the parish. He asked that I help him keep the ministries organized and supported. Beyond that there were no specific duties; this would be a work in progress. There were no predetermined hours and much of the work involved making phone calls. He hoped that I would be willing to do this work until a new pastor arrived. My disability status did not allow me to return to a regular job, but certainly this was an answer to prayer. My skills and experiences could be of use to the church I loved. For a moment, the sting of losing out on ordained ministry was gone.

The great fun of the work was coaching and supporting some of the volunteers in the parish, particularly those who worked with our high schoolers. In those days, Prince of Peace was blessed to have two sisters who had been active as adult sponsors in the high school (Luther League) program. Julie and Lori had worked with Pastor Tim and made the commitment to continue to work with the high schoolers after his departure. Pastor John made the commitment to increase the time he spent with the Luther League, but the preparation of the schedule fell to Julie, Lori, and me.

In this time, the Holy Spirit was at work in Lori's life, drawing her toward a larger vocational calling in the church. We had long talks over large jars of licorice about this new direction for her life. Bible studies were born and a pizza ministry (taking pizza to our high schoolers and their friends on Fridays) grew from Lori's emerging call to ministry. We were having so much fun discovering all that God was doing in our lives.

Months passed and a new pastor was called to the

parish. In the meantime, my mother, sister, and her children had begun worshiping with Pastor Tim as he worked to develop Living Water Lutheran Church. My desire has always been to be an active participant in my home parish, but the commute from my home to Prince of Peace was making that a challenge. It was with a heavy heart that I eventually moved from that first family of faith to join my family of origin in the great adventure with God that is a mission start congregation.

Living Water Lutheran Church began as a wonderful mixture of young families, retirees, and "empty-nesters." In those early days there was always a new baby within our midst who would portray Jesus on Christmas Eve. We grew our own parish. From our very first worship, Pastor Tim allowed (following ELCA guidelines) children to receive the sacrament of Holy Communion as soon as they were physically capable of so doing. The gift of grace was shared with all regardless of our ability to articulate its meaning. That's a good thing, because there are times when I'm not capable of understanding, let alone articulating the meaning of it all. I rest in the power of God's grace to come into my life in this most tangible way.

And I remember chatting with Pastor Tim about the sacramental practice. He and I dreamed of ways to support our children as they grew into an appreciation of God's means of grace. My ministry juices were flowing following those great conversations. From them sprang an idea for a formal role for me in the growth of the ministry of Jesus in and through Living Water Lutheran Church.

Before we could proceed, I had a commitment to complete. I had been elected as the parish's first president and in my four-year tenure we formally organized, completed the purchase of our land, and began construction of the first buildings. My faith had survived leadership; if only barely. Before I could do any other "work" within the parish, I needed to finish my council commitment and rest my business-weary faith.

Pastor Tim understood and the congregation council gave me that time before they offered me the position of director of Faith Formation. Great title. No salary. Just my kind of job. The role was intended to build a ministry structure with programs and resources to support faith development in people of all ages. I was provided a laptop, use of a congregational vehicle, and, most importantly, a supportive environment. Beyond that was a blank slate.

From brainstorming came ideas, which became real in the form of programs. One of those programs was born out of the issue of communing children. "A Place at God's Table" was our effort to help the littlest ones learn about the meal we shared, and God's great gift of grace. I wanted to draw a correlation between God's table and tables in their homes. We did so with an art project to make a special plate and cup for them to use at home. We also prepared food to share. My helpers were unrelated grandmas from the congregation. Parents were given the evening to be on their own. This allowed the children to return home and teach their parents about what they had learned.

Drawing the curriculum and resources together was a most fulfilling endeavor. Pastor Tim, leadership, and the whole people of the congregation were supportive and largely willing to try anything once. As the date of our first offering approached, I was excitedly checking off items from my to-do list. As I made nametags for my helpers, I realized I had a problem. Names like "Grandma Judy" and "Grandma Mary Lee" (yes, I hooked my mother into helping) were clear, but I was stumped as to what to put on my own nametag.

I had no title—I was just Paula. I wasn't really "Aunt Paula," as my niece and nephew had always just called me Paula. When Julie asked them why, they replied, "Well, that's her name!" I did come to understand later that hearing them call me Aunt Paula was a sure indication that they were buttering me up and about to ask for something. Lacking a title had never bothered me, but on that day I was flummoxed.

It was while sharing my quandary with Pastor Tim the question was answered. He suggested "Miss Paula," as this was the manner in which children were instructed to address their preschool teachers. Last names could be challenging to young articulators, therefore first names were preferred.

I liked "Miss Paula." Years earlier (*and I mean many years earlier*), my colleagues at work suggested the nickname "Miss P" for our team T-shirts for our hospital-sponsored New Year's Resolution 10K run and two-mile walk. Our department head asked all of us to participate and promised Bloody Marys and lots of fun. Few of my friends were athletically inclined and not so certain that it would be the least bit fun, but a good Bloody Mary was hard to refuse.

The race was held on New Year's Day. Bright and

early described the race day but not the members of our team. We were, however, looking good in our team shirts. Even in my healthiest years a two-mile walk was a significant challenge. Thankfully, I was among friends with no need to race through the course. Finding and maintaining a reasonable pace was our challenge, finishing was our goal.

Three-quarters of the way into the walk, I knew I was in trouble. Pain medication wasn't holding and my anxiety began to grow. I wondered if I would even finish. My legs were sore and my feet—forget about it—yet my stubborn ego wouldn't allow consideration of quitting. My primary source of discomfort was my elbow. It hurt to walk because of the jarring of the arm. My friends took turns carrying my arm. We all agreed that we were not having the fun we had been promised.

The race pack had long since passed us. We were drifting quickly to the end of the line. The point of no return was long gone so all that was left for us was to continue. One hundred yards from the finish line, we were the next-to-last group on the course. The other was a family walking with their father who, two days earlier, had been discharged from the hospital. One week before that, he had a quadruple bypass surgery. I was racing against a sixty-seven-year-old cardiac rehab patient. His team passed us twenty yards from the finish line.

A new term entered my lexicon that day: DLBF— Dead Last But Finished. That day I had undertaken a task without real knowledge of what it entailed and no assurance that I would be successful. The task had been set before me, and I knew that the only way to succeed in this endeavor was one step at a time. Literally. In order to finish, I had to begin.

Miss P began the race and finished it with a dislocated elbow prosthesis. Would I have begun if I had known for certain the outcome? I doubt it, but, no matter how tempting it is to wonder, it remains most unproductive.

As I reflect for this book I realize that this is a pattern in my life. I'm not the most analytical person you will ever meet. On the contrary, I respond to challenges and opportunities with emotion and passion. Remember, I was in that race because of a social opportunity. On that day "Miss P" became a part of my persona. While "Miss P" takes on things that might give Paula pause, she is that part of me that leaps and trusts things will be all right.

Miss Paula was therefore a natural evolution from Miss P and fit me perfectly. This ministry venture was completely new. It called for that part of me that was willing to leap forward and trust that I would land well.

I had never done any major work with small children. Some might say that it took a pretty big ego to agree to do so without much practical experience. I won't argue that in some respects I am pretty self-confident, but my self-confidence rises and falls depending on the situation. In this regard I think we humans are pretty similar.

Yet, in this new ministry setting my confidence was in the One whose love I was to be teaching. My life's journey had led me to understand that God's great love for me would allow me to reach beyond my own confidence issues and say YES to His calling. Yes, to whatever that calling might entail and wherever it might lead.

Miss Paula became my common name among the

children and many of the adults. My work with faith formation grew to include a little bit of everything. I taught adult Bible studies and, children's Sunday School, began an annual Vacation Bible School, lead a midweek church night, worked with the Altar Guild, and did just about anything else needed to build the ministry. Pastor Tim was a generous supporter. I shall forever be grateful for the way in which he allowed me to have a hands-on experience of ministry.

Pastor Tim was also generous in the way in which he allowed me time in the pulpit. He encouraged me and gave me the chance to hone my preaching skills. He treated me as a genuine partner in ministry.

Work within the church brings with it many headaches and occasional heartaches. This can be said of many kinds of work and most all organizations. Whenever people are involved there is a chance of discord. I have found this to be true in all of the parishes and expressions of the church with which I have worked. Yet, I look back on those times with great joy.

Miss Paula lives on in my current parish. Mother and I bought a new home and moved some distance from Living Water Lutheran Church. Just as I moved from Prince of Peace to Living Water to allow for full participation in the ministry life of my parish, so too I moved from Living Water to Bethany Lutheran Church. Bethany is just five minutes from our house and after worshipping with the people at Bethany we knew we had found our new faith community.

Bethany, like many congregations, has a history of different pastors, sizes of membership, and focuses for ministry. When we joined this small parish, the average age of the membership was over seventy. But these were not your average seventy-year-olds. There was a sense of continued call to do the work of Jesus.

Several years before our arrival, the congregation had been the recipient of a bequest with the specific caveat that the monies be used for youth and family ministry. This senior congregation thought and prayed before saying yes to the gift. Once accepted, the gift was used to develop a facility on the campus, which would serve the new ministry. Children in worship were rare. Although the congregation had long been a sponsor of a Boy Scouts troop and that troop remained active, there was, at the time, no other ministry for young people and their families. Accepting the money from the trust fund was a *Field of Dreams* moment. They prayed: if we build it, they will come.

Honestly, I thought I had left my Miss Paula days behind and wondered if it was time for a new focus. Senior ministry was an interest for me and perhaps Bethany would allow me to explore that with them. It was my intention to share this at the time we gathered with the pastor and other prospective new members.

In the time between the completion of Reynolds Hall (named for the benefactor) Youth and Family Ministry facility and our new member class, two families with two children each came to Bethany. As we sat around tables with our fellow prospective members, Pastor Rick shared some of the hopes and aspirations for the ministry of Bethany. He then asked us for ours. One of the young mothers asked about a program for children. We all chatted about what that program might entail. It sounded very familiar to me.

Pastor Rick said he wasn't sure exactly how, but he said it was worth exploring. Before I could get the words "senior ministry" out of my mouth, I said, "I know how to do that." In an instant, I was outlining all the possibilities and committing myself to the work. A few weeks later, Little Friends of Jesus became the primary ministry for children. Our program of story, music, crafts, and games is where you will find Miss Paula nearly every Wednesday evening. God is Good!

At the end of the day, it matters not whether I am with young or old when doing the work to which I believe the Holy Spirit has called me. My call to ordained ministry had derailed, but the call to share the love of God was alive and well. When seminary was no longer an option, I felt left behind by the Spirit and no longer needed for anything of value in the kingdom of God.

Silly girl, it seemed that God had a bigger vision. As I had shared in a previous chapter, the chance to teach and work with young people literally saved my life and perhaps even my faith. Miss Paula is one of the ways in which God works to bring meaning to my life.

Identity, particularly our identity as Christians, is the topic of many books by much higher-ordered scholarly thinkers than I. I have read only parts of a few of them, because they make identity such a complex issue. Granted, our human identity is complicated, encompassing both science and the humanities.

As Christians, it seems to me that the topic is much more basic. We are simply children of a loving and faithful God. In the manner of children we wander and we make mistakes. We seek to do it our way and speak the words "me" and "mine" all too often. And, like children, we want forgiveness and unconditional love.

In God we have a Father who will not abandon or forsake us. In Jesus we are reminded of His sharing in our human struggles and then assured of the grace and mercy of a loving Father. The Holy Spirit walks with us to remind us who we are and to whom we belong.

Whether our title is mother or father, reverend or padre, saint or sinner, or any of a thousand others, including Miss, our identity is simple. We are, as the old hymn says: children of the Heavenly Father. Thanks be to God!

*Good and gracious God,
Heavenly Father,*

*It is in You we find our identity,
in You we realize the full measure
of grace and mercy.
Call us, we pray, into an ever-evolving
relationship with you so
that we may offer ourselves to your world
as living witnesses of your love.
Help us to remember that when we begin
You are there to help us finish.*

Amen

10

Go With the Flow

*"do not be conformed to this world,
but be transformed by the
renewing of your minds,
so that you may discern what is the will of God…"*

—Romans 12:2 (NRSV)

Have you ever known someone who has been somewhere and/or done something, and returns with a grin like the proverbial Cheshire cat? They are so consumed with their experience that it is literally their sole topic of conversation. And furthermore, despite your mightiest efforts, you just cannot muster anything vaguely approaching their enthusiasm.

Such was the case of my mother and sister following their whitewater river trips. They had such good times and were genuinely anxious to share their joy. Whitewater rafting was not merely a vacation for them, it was a means to experience their passion for the outdoors. Granted, their stories were fun to hear, for a while. Eventually, however, it became my habit to simply smile and nod. It just wasn't an experience I could share. Or so I thought. *(I'm a big fan of indoor plumbing.)*

Remember now, we are talking about my intrepid mother. When she puts her mind to it, there is nothing that will stop her. So when she decided that I needed to go along on a raft trip, arguing the demerits of the decision was pointless. She was going to make it happen. It was time to surrender and go with the flow.

Reservations for these trips must be made one year in advance. Mary Lee was determined that we should go to Idaho and do the "Main Salmon" trip with her outfitter friend Frogg Stewart of Holiday Expeditions (Idaho). Factors influencing her choice were the good weather in central Idaho, the relatively warm water, and few if any bugs. Thank God, few bugs! Making it all the better was Mom's faith that Frogg and his folks could make it work for me.

While I had been raised with a can-do attitude, the reality of my physical limitations had to be addressed. I could do no climbing, hiking, or heavy lifting. *(Aw, shucks.)* This meant that the latrine was going to be a challenge. I also could not get up and down from the ground. This would prove to be an even bigger task, the burden for which would fall to my family members on the trip. These and more considerations had to be acknowledged and then addressed. A bright, happy outlook was not enough. Real planning was essential.

Mother contacted Frogg, who graciously accepted the task of getting Paula down the river. She booked a group reservation, knowing that my Aunt Carol and Uncle Dallas would surely go along with the idea. This would be Dallas' first trip as well. Carol had joined mom a couple of times but Dallas always had health issues that prevented him from doing so. My uncle is a very special man in my life. He has loved me like a father and would do anything he could to make me happy. His health had been in tough shape for many years. In fact, we often said he had more lives than a cat. From a multiple coronary artery bypass surgery in the 1970s to allergies and skin/rash problems, he had faced the gamut. Following repeated bouts of severe ulcerative colitis, he was forced to have a colectomy. And there was more. Suffice it to say, he had as much hospital experience as I.

Dallas also has an indomitable spirit. He is as friendly as a puppy and has never met a stranger. More than willing to share his story, he could tell details of his life to almost anybody. Sometimes, this could be uncomfortable to the rest of us. With all that said, however, I love him so very much.

This would be a genuine family-and-friends experience. The planning made for growing excitement. Even though the trip was nearly a year away, I was excited at the possibilities.

A month away from departure, my feelings began to change. Yes, I was excited about the trip, but my anxiety meter began to inch upward. It was all about the usual stuff. How will I handle the whole outdoor experience and the absence of creature comforts? I have often said, "My idea of roughing it is a hotel without room service." Sleeping on the ground and pretending that an old ammo can with a wooden seat is a toilet were chief among my anxieties. Mother asked me to trust her and did all she could to assure and reassure me. Clearly I was going and it was time to "get over it."

We assembled all the necessary gear, packed up, and began the long drive to Boise, Idaho. Once in Boise, we would connect with the river guides and the adventure would begin. YIPPEEE!

The night before we left Boise for the river, we had an instructional session with one of our river guides. We were each issued two black rubber river bags and shown the proper way to load the bag and, more importantly, how to close it. When closed properly, the bag is watertight. The guide told us that the waterproofing of our stuff meant we'd have dry clothes at night. Most of the time, things should be all right but it would be all so important on "BIG WATER DAY." There was that phrase: BIG WATER DAY. We would hear it over and over again. And each time my anticipation grew.

Cars, airplanes, and a bus were needed to get us to our water excursion. Taxis shuttled our equipment and us from the hotel to the airport where we boarded several small (four to eight-passenger) aircraft for a flight from Boise to Salmon, Idaho. We traveled over some of God's most beautiful creation. From the air, the mountains and the trees seemed so close that we could have reached out and touched them. The vista from the aircraft was awesome even for a white-knuckle flier like me.

When we landed in Salmon, the one and only Frogg Stewart greeted us. The first thing I noticed about Frogg was his broad smile. He greeted my mother like they were long-lost relatives. Hugs and laughter abounded. Frogg is a man of average height, with a belly that suggests perhaps one too many beers have been consumed along the way. He is by no means fat. Rather, he appeared tanned and strong. He has a beard and some scruffy hair that leaks out of the bottom of his baseball cap. In many respects he looks like an old hippie who has found a way to make a living in the great outdoors.

When we were introduced, Frogg threw his arms around me and hugged me and said, "I've waited a long time to meet you, my dear." Apparently Mother had been telling some stories on her previous trips. As we talked, he made it very clear that he and his staff had committed to make my river trip a memorable one. I found this most reassuring.

For the last leg of our trip, we loaded onto an old school bus for the several-hour drive to the "put-in" where we met our boats and guides. Once again, we experienced some extraordinarily beautiful country. The bus ride from Salmon passed through some stunning scenery. I found myself looking from one side to the other, afraid that I would miss seeing something along the way. During this portion of the trip my perspective shifted. Riding through the woods and occasionally alongside the meandering river, the wilderness component of the trip became very real to me. When I caught my first look at the river, I became giddy like a schoolgirl. *Am I really ready to do this? Oh yes, I am!*

Our bus stopped one last time at a country general store where we loaded up on beer, pop, and snacks. There was plenty of food provided by the outfitter, but these were our personal stashed goodies. And there is never enough beer because it is said to be bad luck to run out of beer on the river. Once back on the bus for the bumpy ride down to the river and our boats, it was time for our first beer. The trip had begun.

We arrived at the launch site, and everyone began to unload the bus. People were so kind. My stuff came off the bus and was carried down to the boats without me asking. Our guides were working on their boats while all the stuff was brought down.

I found a rock that was tall enough for me to sit on. I found it hard to focus as I looked around and saw all that was going on around me. It was akin to watching a giant anthill. There was another trip with a different outfitter loading right next to us. The setting was beautiful and the sound of the river sent a current through my body. I realized that I was excited and happy to be there.

Frogg joined the other two guides down on their boats. Pulling on ropes and tying knots, they prepared so methodically. Soon, a tall, slender man hopped off the boat and called to us to gather around. His name is Malcolm and he looked like he spent most of his life in the outdoors eating nuts and berries. The red hair and beard completed the picture. He introduced himself as our trip leader, and then to Sarah as the other guide. She was young and beautiful and he told us she was a rookie. This was Sarah's first season on the river.

Malcolm began our pre-trip instruction assigning each of us proper life jackets. They were to be worn on the boats at all times and regularly checked to ensure they were snapped securely. Life jackets, or more accurately personal flotation devices (PFD), were critical for our safety.

Next, Malcolm reviewed the black bag procedure, restating the imperative that they be rolled and buckled snugly. To emphasize his point, he grabbed one of the black bags lined up to be loaded onto the boats. "This will never do," he began. "A person with this bag may not have wet clothes tonight, but they will for sure after BIG WATER DAY." He unbuckled the bag and refolded it in the proper manner.

We were invited to get our bags and reseal them. I think Mother and I were the only ones who did not have to redo our bags. She was a pro and had done mine for me.

There were a few more rules of the river and then time to load up. The three guides stood on their boats and we threw them black bags to tie into their load as they called for them. In short order we were on the boats and looking back at the shore.

We were headed down the *River of No Return*. This nickname comes from early expeditions, most famously Lewis and Clark, who realized that its swift current, occasional low water levels, and rocky bed made travel possible in one direction only: down. It wasn't until much later, with the advent of jet boats, that the river could be navigated against the current. *River of No Return* is also the title of a 1954 movie directed by Otto Preminger, and starring Robert Mitchum and Marilyn Monroe. Thankfully, I had not seen it prior to our trip.

We had just begun when we hit some turbulence. The boat rocked a bit and I giggled with glee. My mother quickly told me these were simply "riffles" and not rapids. OMG! This was going to be great! Actually, I think I embarrassed her with my rookie exuberance. I was embarrassed when, later that day, we actually experienced real rapids.

Our first night's stop was at the most picturesque beach I'd ever seen. It was a beautiful, long sandy beach with plenty of room for the kitchen, tents, and volleyball. The forest came down to the sand and brought with it wonderfully flat walking areas. There was even a small rocky area at the river shore that provided a great place for bathing. Bathing on a river trip involves an interesting blend of creativity, bravery, trust, and immodesty. Creativity comes in finding ways to get to a place in the river where the water is deep enough (to cover your body while you clean) and yet current is not strong enough to pull you off your feet. Bravery is a part of that, but also is needed to dunk your head under cold water to rinse out the shampoo.

From my perspective, trust and immodesty must go hand in hand. On the river there exists this code of conduct that basically boils down to "Mind your own business." Some bathe in their swimsuits and others do so in the nude. There are no large group baths, or at least I have never been a part of one. Almost everyone finds a way to wrap in a towel and get out of his or her suit as they exit the water. Everyone is entitled to have their experience, and short of purely offensive or dangerous behavior, people are cordially invited to look the other way. We trust this standard and swallow our modesty in order to experience the simple joy of cleanliness.

Dinner was cooked (in those days) over an open fire. Our guides were wonderful cooks. That first night set the tone for all the fabulous meals that followed. More than great cooks, our guides were wonderful hosts. They seemed genuinely interested in making our experience complete both on and off the river. After dinner there were adult beverages (beer, wine in the box, and other spirits from our stop at the General Store) and great conversation around the campfire. Frogg was often the center of attention, sharing stories and lore from the river. He was a terrific storyteller and I hated to see the evening end. Our time as a group around the campfire concluded with some final directions from Malcolm. He advised that we get some rest, as the next day would be full. The rapids would be bigger so make certain to seal your black bags properly. After all, he reminded us, it would be good practice for Day 3, also known as BIG WATER DAY.

Sleeping in a tent was not a great experience for my body. Sand is really pretty hard and, although I had an air mattress, it was still tough. But the sound of the river was so soothing that sleep came more readily than I had feared. We awakened in the morning to the crackle of a fire and the smell of coffee. Glorious!

My body brought challenges to this experience. No delicate way to put it: I had to have assistance anytime I needed to "toilet." We had been told to pee in the river and poop in the can. The can, literally an old ammo can with a wooden toilet seat, was strategically located a safe distance from the camp. I needed help getting to either place. And when the urge came in the middle of the night, I also needed help getting up and down from the ground. Thank God for my mother and my aunt. They were there for me, without complaint, whenever I needed. *(Lord, I am so blessed!)*

The challenge was to swallow my misplaced pride and set aside my overwhelming need for independence and allow people to help me. Choices are often less complicated than we make them. I could choose to happily and thankfully take the gracious assistance offered and enjoy my trip. Or, I could turn inward, resentful and ashamed that I needed help, and in so doing miss the opportunity to appreciate the journey. Either way, I wasn't going five days without "toileting."

Choosing to be happy has been an important part of my life. Not much about my body (up to that point) had been within my control. All that remained was my choice about how I would react. Attitude proved to be the difference for me. Somehow my whole life seemed to be preparation for this trip, and the trip proceeded with gusto. Each new rapid was more delightful than the one before. Each meal was an unexpected culinary treat. We were constantly reminded by the guides of the need to wear our PFDs snugly and to close our black bags tightly.

Throughout the second day we were treated to the stories and interpretational wisdom of our guides. With each passing hour (it seemed) they coaxed more anticipation of BIG WATER DAY. Throughout camp that night the stories grew even larger.

Day 3—BIG WATER DAY—had finally arrived. Malcolm was far more insistent that we have our gear in good order. What had seemed playful before was now serious business. Clearly the mood had changed. Even Frogg seemed different to me. Still laughing and joking a bit, he was also serious about rigging the boats for the day's adventure. Frogg had always been the epitome of professionalism, yet he was also quite relaxed and at ease. Years of being on the river had given him that sense.

Frogg and the other guides wore a different style of PFD. Theirs were double zipped and cinched on the sides. They always wore them. I was sure that I had seen, on a couple of occasions, Frogg head through a small rapid with his PFD only partially zipped. I told myself this was because he knew this river. He didn't take risks lightly but knew when it would be important to be double zipped.

Each morning there was a kind of dance among the guests to determine in which boat they would ride. BIG WATER DAY made that dance a bit more frenetic.

Mother's intuition combined with her river experience made her keenly aware of the need to declare early. "I think you should ride with Frogg today," she said. "I'll go with Sarah, but I'd feel better if you ride with Frogg."

"Okay." I had ridden with mother earlier in the trip so it all seemed fine to me. Frogg was so much fun, I felt lucky to do BIG WATER DAY with him.

Putting your personal ammo can on the boat of your choice reserved your place. Mother put mine on Frogg's. Behind her came Carol with her can as well as Dallas's can. Remember, I adore Carol and Dallas, but in that moment my heart sank just a bit. My overwhelming concern was for Dallas and his health. Would we become the hospital barge? How would this affect our much-anticipated BIG WATER DAY? I chose to hold my concern aside. Mom knew, but there was no value in making it public. Partly because I was more than a bit ashamed of myself, I also did not want to hurt Dallas or Carol.

Bags checked. PFDs buckled. We set off for the BIG WATER DAY about which we had heard so much.

It didn't take long for the difference in this day to become obvious. As we approached our first big rapid the guides pulled the boats to shore. Once tied down, they would hike down river and up onto whatever rise they could find in order to "scout" the rapid. Once they had determined the path they would run they returned to the boats. Off we would go.

Early on, most guests waited in the boats while the guides were scouting. With each rapid, a few more would venture out of the boat in order to follow their guide and get a view of the coming ride.

Dallas and I never left our boat. The chatter that we experienced from the others made us feel the excitement ourselves. I felt a little left out, but that is sometimes just part of my life's journey. Still, in the back of my mind lurked the question of whether or not the guides were thinking of us differently because of our health issues. But, oh how the joy of running the rapid would force the negative thoughts out of my mind.

When we stopped for lunch, there was more than the normal chatter around the group. Reliving the morning's rapids from others' perspectives was great. Sometimes I wondered if we had all been on the same river because individual experiences were so unique. Fascinating!

"Is there more big water?" Everyone wondered. I asked.

"Oh yes!" was the nearly choral response of the guides.

"Wait until they see Salmon Falls." The twinkle in Frogg's eyes said all that I needed to know. This was going to be the one. This was what this trip had prepared me to experience.

Salmon Falls is, like all rapids, different, based on the water level of the river. It is so named because there is a drop from the top to the bottom. "Falls" are that way. It just sounded almost magical to me. I could hardly wait!

Now it was time—the one I had waited for—Salmon Falls. Again, Frogg's demeanor shifted to more "strictly business."

Malcolm led the boats to shore. As the guides tied us securely to the rocks, I was caught by the sound in the air. It was loud, and yet not a scary kind of loud. The sound made by the river wrapped around us like a blanket and pushed the rest of my world away. It really was magical.

Sometimes in my moments of darkness and/or despair, I recall that time. Sitting on the boat, the sun warm on my face, the air cool on my skin, and that beautiful sound. The cares of the present are silenced by the memory of that glorious moment.

Once again all of the guests followed the guides up on the rocks to get a view of the river. Because of the falls, it is essential to climb up to see the entire run, as it is not visible from the water level. Failure to accurately assess and plan your run could result in severe damage to body and/or boat.

Dallas and I could almost hear them scouting in the distance. Frogg's voice worked that way. What we could not hear, we could see. Frogg and Malcolm, with Sarah sandwiched in the middle, pointed emphatically. Oh, what was about to happen? My mind was racing.

As they began to return to us, we really could hear Frogg. He was telling Sarah that she must take the run "right straight down the middle." He added, "Follow Malcolm and take it right straight down the middle." If he said it once, he said it half a dozen times.

The returning guests were uncharacteristically quiet. There was no bravado from them. In its place there was a sort of anxious calm. You know the feeling that leads you to say to yourself "Easy does it. You can do this." They climbed into their boats and tightened their PFDs.

Frogg was now standing on our boat barking to the other two guides now in their boats. "Malcolm goes first. Wait till you see him downstream, then Sarah you go, right straight down the middle." I was so ready to go until Frogg's next statement. "I'm going to take Paula and Dallas down the left." My heart sank.

The emotions of that moment tumbled around my

mind. I was disappointed that I was going to miss the fun, the thrill of that center run. Having come this far, why was I being cheated out of the full experience? When I started asking "Why," I knew that my personal pity party was in full swing.

Mary Lee had taught me the term "cheater run." It is a run that avoids the more dangerous path in favor of a safer, easier one. I was convinced that this was what was happening here. The left side of Salmon Falls was the cheater run.

Our three-boat flotilla pulled out into the middle of the river. Malcolm and his group were in front. Sarah the rookie, with my mother on board, was in second position. Frogg was "pulling sweep" as the last boat.

Malcolm stood up in his boat on the lip of the rapid. His tall, lean frame appeared rather like a beacon. I wanted so desperately to be on his boat.

And the pity party continued. Once I felt sorry enough for myself, I turned to resentment of others. I had decided in that instant that it was Dallas's fault. Frogg was afraid for Dallas and his bad heart and so chose to take the cheater run because of him. Resentment is like the proverbial rolling stone, growing rapidly by gathering in on itself. I determined that it had nothing to do with me; it was now all about Dallas. Mind you, all of this is happening in splits of seconds. Runaway emotions are like that.

I watch as Malcolm's boat goes over the edge and into the rapids. Whooping and hollering from the guests could have been heard in Boise. It was such a happy noise. When we saw them again they were on smooth water, celebrating their great run.

"Just like that," Frogg yelled to Sarah. "Take her right

straight down the middle!" *Blah, blah, blah.* If I had to hear "right straight down the middle" one more time, I was going to puke.

Sarah squared her boat into the tongue of the rapid, and with a heavy grunt, she and her guests disappeared from our line of sight. Their gleeful emanations at least meant that my mother was having a great run. Their reunion with Malcolm's boat was cause for further celebration.

As I returned to my pity party, Frogg's voice broke my focus. He said, "Hey, Paula, how tightly can you hang on?" My emotional switch flipped. Hope flooded into the barren land of my self-pity.

"Tightly, very well, I can handle it," I must have blubbered. I had to convince Frogg that I could do it.

Then Frogg asked the same question of Dallas. Quick prayer: Dallas, please don't ruin this for me. It is not pretty to tell, but I was completely self-consumed. This was all about me in that moment. Dallas told Frogg that he was good and prepared to hang on. *YES! I knew I loved that man!*

But Frogg kept moving the boat across the river toward the left. I had been so sure that we had convinced Frogg we could do it that I could not understand why we were moving farther away from the middle run and heading for the cheater run on the left.

Three, perhaps five, seconds later, I was resigned to what little I could get from the "cheater." Having ridden in the front of the boat all day, I took the position of eyes forward and the attitude of "go with the flow." The peace of mind was a welcome relief from the emotional acrobatics of the last twenty minutes.

My newly found blissful peace was interrupted

once again. There was a sound I had not heard before. ZIP. Frogg was zipping his PFD—twice. Then came the sound of him securing the side clamps. Something was clearly not as I had thought. Why would Frogg be securing his PFD for a cheater run? Perhaps I had been mistaken.

"Take hold of those ropes, kids, because here we go!"

In a flash, we were over the edge and I couldn't see the bottom of the river. Our boat was nearly perpendicular to the water. Just as suddenly, we hit something like a shelf of water and we were launched, airborne! Our brief flight was the most outrageous experience of my life.

Truthfully, I don't remember much of the rest of the run. What I do recall is that I was shouting (sometimes expletives, I'm sad to admit) throughout the run. It was freaking amazing!

Through the final waves of the rapid, we now headed to the other boats for celebration. There was much cheering and high fives all around. We looked back up the river to the place from whence we came. I was on such an adrenaline rush that it almost seemed unreal. Middle or left hardly mattered.

Frogg maneuvered the boat around so that I could see my mom. Everyone else was cheering and she had tears in her eyes.

"Mama, don't cry, please. I had a wonderful time."

"Oh honey," she said. "You don't understand." She proceeded to explain that Frogg had given me an amazing gift. Very few people get a chance to run the left side of Salmon Falls. Sometimes it is just plain not runnable. She told me, "You'll always be able to say you ran Salmon Falls on the left."

She knew what I had; now so did I.

There were more rapids, more camps, and more wonderful memories on that trip. That first trip whets my appetite for the river and all the experiences that a trip would entail. Relationships have a unique intimacy when on the river. Everyone has bad hair days and nobody watches the clock.

The river and the canyons it runs through create a cathedral. God is ever so present to me in that place. From the quiet of the night to the roar of the river, the sound of the grouse to the butting of ram antlers, it all comes together like a symphony. Many people have waxed far more eloquently than I about the river. Now, their poetry is personal.

Since then I have made three other trips down the main Salmon. Each trip is as unique as the river itself. Something always captures my heart. Never again have I, nor anyone else on the trip, run the left side of Salmon Falls.

Oh, by the way: Long before it was used by other vacation sites, we were taught this by our river guides: What happens on the river…stays on the river.

To that I simply add: Thanks be to God—AMEN!

There is an interesting phenomenon on the river called an "eddy." An eddy is where the current actually runs backward. Eddies occur in the middle of the river, but most frequently they run closer to the shoreline. They may be trouble or they can be a safe place to rest and collect oneself before continuing. The calm of an eddy allows time to look back at where you have been and forward toward your destination.

Caution! Eddies can also be sticky places from which to escape. Other debris may be stuck in the eddy that may complicate your time there and make your exit difficult. The professionals on the river know how and when to "catch an eddy" for their purposes. This is using what the river will give them to make the journey a good one.

Frequently the river is a metaphor for life in general. I believe this to be true. The river is a living thing and as such is ever changing. Powerful in the extreme, the river can be slowed but never fully stopped. A dammed river may be slowed but, unless the dam is diligently maintained, the water will ultimately break through.

Such is life, ever changing. Our life has a powerful desire to keep on. It is the nature of our God-given human spirit. We navigate life as we do the river, never fully in control of our circumstance, yet always able to move through the water, take the rapids and, when needed, catch an eddy or two.

So, do you know where the eddies in your life exist? What are the places, or who are the people, that allow you the time and space to rest, reflect, and recharge? Are there things that keep you from your needed "eddy" moments? Why?

I am thinking of that wonderful Chapter 12 in Paul's letter to the Romans where he writes:

> *"do not be conformed to this world,*
> *but be transformed by the renewing of your minds,*
> *so that you may discern what is the will of God—*
> *what is good and acceptable and perfect."* (NRSV)

Sometimes our life (our river) can be quite overwhelming. We can be consumed by it all. Here is Paul inviting us to be transformed by God's Spirit rather than conformed to what the world offers us. Yes, it is often easier said than done, but...

Consider this. Jesus is our ever-present eddy, a place and a person in whom we may rest, reflect, and recharge. In Him we have a safe place to see where we have been and a glorious place to look forward.

*Good and gracious God,
Creator of the universe,
For the majesty of Your creation
for mountains and valleys, forests, and deserts,
and the trees and plants and flowers which adorn it all,
for life-giving water which nourishes our bodies
and provides us opportunity to recreate and travel,
for the times we have merely placed our feet in a pond,
explored in a creek, swam in a lake or floated down a river,
for the chance to meet You in all these places,
and for finding time to rest, reflect and recharge,
I give You thanks and praise.*

Amen

11

"Just a Bunch of Church HAGS"

*"You can dance, you can jive, having the time of your life
See that girl, watch that scene, diggin' the dancing queen…"*

"Dancing Queen" by Abba

Road Trip!

No, this is not a story of my misspent youth, not that I am admitting to anything.... Rather, it is a story of my better-spent adulthood.

The story really began weeks earlier when Mother and I bought a new GMC Suburban. We did so in hopes that we could travel safely and comfortably in a vehicle with a reputation for all that plus durability. That sounds so mature, but, honestly, it was a sweet ride! This was no ordinary, off-the-assembly-line 'burb. It was a conversion vehicle, meaning it had been redone with all sorts of nice appointments. With my first sniff of the oversized, premium-leather captain's seats, I was sold. Top that with a TV/VCR, a primo stereo, and way-cool Nerf-style step bars—okay—I was obsessed. It was my first cool car.

More than anything, I wanted to hit the road in my super-cool party wagon. The goal was a getaway with friends. My intention was for laughter, lots of laughter, and to feel only joy and bliss. Oh, and of course, it would be a time of food and beverage. I had no trouble convincing myself that this trip would be my personal Great Escape.

Two years of painful uncertainty had finally come to an end. My arm was now repaired; at least to the extent possible. There was no miraculous return of function in the damaged radial nerve. Available legal remedies, although not technically exhausted, were at least settled. Finished.

I had come to a STOP sign on the road of life. A turn onto a new stretch of road was in order. Left or right did not matter so much. A move, any move, meant progress.

I was exhausted from the stillness of life. Holding still is much more difficult than it appears. First of all, it's boring. Secondly, it's just damn painful, sometimes physically, and sometimes emotionally. Each day presented a struggle for even a modicum of independence. It is very difficult to explain how painful swelling and numbness is, for those who have not had the experience. Nerves work overtime to find their partners and skin is stretched to tenderness. This was my stillness, my "same old, same old." Anything new was a welcome diversion. Consequently, the idea of this trip began to be symbolic of a new moment in my life.

What did I want in this new moment? I am not entirely certain that I can effectively explain. I knew I wanted to be happy. Doesn't everyone? It seems nearly impossible to define "happy." I believe that I will know it when I feel it. I suppose this is a universal experience. Much as "beauty is in the eye of the beholder," happiness may only be experienced by the happy.

Perhaps there was even more that I wanted, but surely

before happy I needed contentment. It was an awful lot to ask from a car trip. Contentment can be an elusive creature, sort of the Loch Ness monster of personal zen. Many are certain that it exists, or in this case can be attained, but not so many have ever really seen or found it. In the months preceding our trip, I had struggled on the fence post between despair and hope. Contentment seemed to be the oasis in the distance. We see it, or so we think. Yet it is often so far beyond our reach.

In those days as well, God's consolation seemed just beyond my reach. My spirit was bruised by the struggle. All too often, in the manner of a petulant child, my prayers came with kicking and screaming; "Oh God—I don't like this—make it go away!"

And in a process that defies time and specificity, through the weakness of the wounded heart, my Lord held me in his arms until my prayer became: "Here I am, Lord—I am broken—I surrender—I am tired of the battle. I don't know what to do. If there is to be life made from this mess, it will be you, Lord, not I who triumphs and shines through."

God did, as always, know the truth. My prayers were open and honest. When struggling, it is important to remember that God's arms are wide and His ability to bear our despair as well as lift it is infinite.

The rest of the story, and perhaps even the real story, is that I was emotionally incapable of sharing the full truth of my circumstances. To the world, I appeared to be bravely pressing on through all life's challenges. "You are so courageous," people would say. My reply was polite, "Thank you, you are too kind." Beyond my family, no one knew the full story.

The road trip was, on the surface, a celebration. New

car. New direction on life's road. New friendships. For me it was a chance to change venues and, perhaps, get a real break from my inner struggle. Now was the time for joy and peace, especially peace of mind.

With all of that serving as a backdrop, having the idea for the trip was only a small part of the process. There were details to be addressed—little things like where to go and, more importantly, who to invite along.

Sharing my dream with my friend Reid was the first step. Together we planned (*well, sort of like plotted*) and began to determine the lucky winners of the four remaining seats in the Suburban. The six seats were filled by an act of the Holy Spirit. Reid and I may have thought we were in charge, but once again, the power of God to enter our lives in the most unlikely ways became apparent. We were blessed to have many women in our lives who would have been delightful companions on our great adventure. Yet as we talked, and especially as we prayed, the names of the women we were to invite became so very clear to both of us. These women had never been together as a regular group although most had been together in some group or function. Some had longer or deeper personal connections, but we all had two critical things in common: 1) We loved the Lord, and 2) We were nervous about spending the time together and especially about sharing a bathroom.

With trust in item number one, and setting aside item number two, these beautiful women said yes.

Seat number one was mine—but I suppose you have already guessed that!

Seat number two belonged to my partner in crime, Reid. Intelligent, articulate, and compassionate, Reid has the greatest capacity for friendship of anyone I've ever known. She took to this task immediately because she is a party waiting to happen. What I didn't know is how well she could mix a cocktail. *(Her rum and cokes are the best!)* We had a sort of life cycle to our relationship. There were struggles. Perhaps because she knows me best, I too readily will pull back when I am fighting my inner demons. And, in all honesty, she is much better at being a friend than I. With patience and love, she has forgiven me and we are, as I write, in a wonderful place. She is my very dear friend.

Seat number three went to Reid's very longtime friend, Lana. Lana is a first grade teacher. This is not just her job. I've come to understand that it sums up her essence. Lana was born and raised in Arkansas; the girl knows her Elvis music and can cook! She and her family had only recently begun worshiping with us, but Reid was certain that she would fit right into the mix. Reid is brilliant, Lana fit like God had chosen her. Oh, that's right—He did.

Jane took seat number four. There were many ways that we knew of Jane, but for me it was her sons who made the connection. Both Wiley and Wes had been my Confirmation students. Her older son, Wiley, turned out to be important in our group identity. More on that later. Jane is beautiful on the outside, but even more so on the inside. Sometimes she is the quiet one in the bunch, and then there are the times we can't get her off the dance floor.

Seat number five was for Kris. Reid and I suspected that Kris had the kind of sense of humor necessary for this kind of trip. And after all, six women in one vehicle really called for comic relief. Both of us had been in classes and/or studies with Kris (and her family). Kris is an amazing storyteller with a gift for making us laugh. She also has the best mind for movie, music, cultural, TV, you-name-it trivia of anyone I know. She is my "phone a friend" if I am ever a contestant on *Who Wants to Be a Millionaire?*

For seat number six, Reid and I chose Shirley. The three of us had been meeting regularly for prayer and time of discipleship. Shirley, like the others, had had interactions with the other gals through church. We appreciated her deeply faithful and compassionate heart, but it didn't hurt that she was also an accountant. Managing the money in a group situation is never fun, therefore it's always good to carry a professional.

So now we have a group and the question becomes—WHERE and WHEN. Like all good Arizonans, our first thought in the summer heat is San Diego, California. Thanks to the generosity of another couple from church (my friends R & A), we had an amazing home in La Jolla for our three-day getaway. Our destination was a beach house in LaJolla, California. Not bad! When I think back on our trip, I find myself so amazingly grateful. The blessings of these new friends would be revealed in good time.

Richard and Alice are my longstanding friends. I have served on church councils with Alice, even worked for her for a brief time. She is a role model for strong women. I am awed by her compassion. Her wisdom has been a gift to me many, many times. Richard is the consummate example of a successful man. While the world may see "The Chairman," those fortunate to know him see more: a playful spirit coupled with a great sense of humor, a loving father and spouse, and most powerfully, a man of deep and abiding faith.

Richard and Alice gave us a place to stay and so much more. Their gift was the chance to breathe the sea air, and listen to waves crashing on the beach, to watch the beautiful surfers change clothes on the street in front of the house (*mmm*), and to stay up late into the night, talking and listening, a place to form friendships. I doubt that I have ever really told the two of them how much I love them, and how much we appreciated the gift they gave us. By the time this is published, I will have done so in person.

Each of us made arrangements for our work and home commitments, and the trip was set. There was a modest amount of anxiety as we gathered, pre-launch, at Reid's. Months later, we all admitted to a bit of trepidation about a car trip with a new circle of friends. I am convinced that the Holy Spirit once again was active in the formation of our group. We had a shared faith and some shared experiences, but we would not likely have been together in such a way if left to our own devices.

So there we stood in the driveway at Reid's house. The Suburban was loaded, photos taken, and our anxieties and hopes were safely in hand. Prayer had been pivotal in our formation and continues to be the constant through all our times together. Holding hands and praying together set the tone for our trip. I found myself praying for peace and ease, two things missing from my current circumstance, and, I feared, almost impossible to achieve in a group of women together for the first time. Yet again, I hear the Lord laughing, reminding me that: *"in all things God works for the good of those who love him…"* (Romans 8:28) or, as my mother would say: "Oh ye of little faith."

Once in the car and on the road, the laughter

began. Kris's sense of humor more than lived up to our expectations. She had us snorting and wetting pants before we hit Gila Bend. *(If you are not familiar with Arizona geography, either find a map or just trust me that we were bonding as a group immediately.)* One word or phrase from one of her stories would send us back into rails of laughter. To this day, "farty-pants" is the favored curse word in our group.

The details of our trip are almost irrelevant. Suffice to say we ate, drank, laughed, cried, danced, and slept in the cool ocean air. We became friends and began to live into our mutual calling as sisters in Christ.

For me the time served as I had prayed it would. Somewhere between the ice cream and the laughter, and almost without my noticing, the layers of pain began to peel away. The burden I had been carrying seemed lighter. I would love to tell you that in our circle of fellowship, I opened up and shared myself on a grand level. I did not. I would, I think, like to tell you that the Lord spoke to me during a walk on the beach. Didn't happen.

What did happen is profound in its simplicity. My inner strife and turmoil was soothed by my external relationships. It was hard to lament my situation when I was with people who were making me laugh. We laughed and we danced. It is not only impossible to dance when focused on what you can't do, it is downright embarrassing. My gaze was raised and the horizon looked so much better than the rough ground beneath me.

People. Life. Laughter. Looking forward. These are not new concepts, my friends, but the actual experience of them was. The realization came that I spent more time looking at what was going wrong in my own life, and I failed to recognize all the powerful love that was present as well.

In the lives of the women around me, I found hope—hope that the "same old same old" was a thing of the past. Between these women and the Holy Spirit of God, my life had taken that much-hoped-for turn in the road.

We tried many times during that first trip to create a group name. Perhaps it was the near-instant bonding, or the rum and coke, or perhaps the echoes of schoolgirl cliques, but we knew we needed a name. Most of the options identified in San Diego were not so good *(see previous reference to rum and coke)*, so try as we might, we left without a name.

Each of us returned home anxious to share with our families (and pretty much anyone who would listen) our joy in discovering new friendships. The exception of course, that great sacred honor and trust which is held in the rule: "What happens in Vegas, stays in Vegas," or for us "What happens in La Jolla, stays in La Jolla."

Jane told us the story of her sharing with her family. Her enthusiasm was momentarily derailed when her son Wiley said, "Oh, Mom, you guys are just a bunch of church hags." As she shared that story with us in our next gathering we had a corporate aha moment. We laughed out loud. Some of us laughed so hard, we needed a change of underwear.

HAGS—Church HAGS—we finally had a name! We were delighted to embrace what might appear to others to be the unembraceable. Lord, as I'm writing this,

I'm beginning to think we sound like Jesus followers. Imagine that!

Church, our faith community, had been our common starting place. That's no lie. *(It's a good thing, Martha.)* So, the word "church" fit.

One look into the mirror made denying the term HAG unrealistic. Certainly we weren't hags like Halloween witches. We were seasoned women. We bore the marks of aging, and we did so beautifully and gracefully.

Oh, and another thing: we proclaim Jesus as Lord and Savior. Jesus, the one who touched the untouchable, forgave the sinners, and embraced the un-embraceable—*hum*—sounds like a role model to me. Sounds like church HAGS. I think Jesus would approve.

HAGS we were! Further, we consider HAGS to be an acronym. To know this group is to understand that we are: Heavenly Angels—God Sent.

We have continued to meet, regularly sharing the journey together. Prayer is the constant hallmark of our group. Continuing to travel together at least once a year enables us to keep our bathroom-sharing skills up to speed. We even have a theme song. It is "Dancing Queen" by Abba. It serves the dual purpose of group bonding and sharing the public embarrassment when we dance together. It's worth it (to me) every time.

Shortly after our return from California, it became apparent that we had failed to include one very important young HAG. Julie became a part of our group right after our trip to Maui. Yeah, the timing was not so good. The youngest member of our group, she is now in charge of remembering everything. As we age, we thought it was good to have that covered. Moreover, she is the embodiment of life and laughter, with a nice dose of style. I rather enjoyed not being the only single woman in the group.

In the succeeding years, our group has grown to include other women. Each has brought their beautiful heart, passion for the Lord, and unique spirit. Shirley has moved to Minnesota. *(Yeah, we thought that way also.)* Our families have had weddings and babies, and have been tested by divorces and career changes. Friendships have been strained and grown stronger. We have faced cancer and, by the grace of God, are still standing. Lots of life. Lots of prayers. We think all little girls want to grow up to be church HAGS. God is so good!

It is the HAGS who, on more than one occasion, have arrived at my door armed with casseroles and toilet brushes. Only your best friends will do your laundry, clean your toilets, and pick up dog poop. The HAGS have dressed and undressed me without laughing. They sit with my family while I'm in the operating room and then make the post-op calls to other friends.

More important to me than all that *(I know, what could be better than a friend who cleans your toilets?)* is they have the most beautifully tuned vision. At once they are able to see my limits, my physical challenges and needs. And in the next instant, they gracefully look beyond them to see me! Not the arthritis, not the missing leg, just me! This is the most profound gift they give me.

I am certain there is something in each of us that we want to be seen or heard by those who love us. What is it in your life?

Take some time to examine your circumstances. Look with "accountable" eyes on the things that give you joy and those that bring despair. Perhaps there is even something that grinds you to a more halting tempo in life. Hopefully there is something that makes you dance.

Look at the relationships in your life. Consider how you show yourself to those most dear to you. Do they have "HAG vision" and see all of you? Do *you* allow them to see all of you, to know all of you?

As I write this, I hear the voice of my teacher, a special man named David, saying, "Be accountable in your life. If there is something you wish to share, do it. Your relationships grow based on what you put into them." Those words were difficult to hear the first time he said them to me. Not a whole lot easier the hundredth time he said them to me. But they are true. Don't tell David, but I think he is a wise man.

When we take off our mask of the day and come before God, we do so with confidence that He sees *us*. He sees and knows us all, completely. He will enable us to share ourselves, first with Him, and then with those we love and care for. This is the Grace of God!

*Good and gracious God,
Companion on our journey,*

*Give peace to those who read this chapter.
Shine on their path so that they
may journey from despair to light.
Place around them people who
lovingly and gracefully see them and support them.*

And, as always, much love to my girls—the HAGS!

Amen.

12

Hey, Now I'm a Rock Star

"For I know the plans I have for you, declares the Lord,
plans to prosper you and not to harm you,
plans to give you hope and a future."

—Jeremiah 29:11

I lead a blessed life. I mean that quite sincerely. You have read of my struggles and health issues, so I'm not trying to make light of them in this chapter. To the contrary, I want to share with you the moments that led me to a true and full acceptance and, more than that, a joy about my life.

Life and all its circumstances can either overwhelm you or launch you. I have always been puzzled, even intrigued, by the differences in the way people meet challenges and live their lives. Sociologists and psychologists have studied this for years and published a variety of findings, which attempt to explain our human differences in the way we act and react. Our differences range from our family support systems to ethnic origins to faith-based belief systems. And I'm certain there are others.

For me, life has always been about taking each moment in stride. Whether I knew that overtly or not I don't recall. But somewhere between my mother telling me to "figure out a way to get my socks on by myself" to the alarm going off, forcing me to get up and get to work, the reality of life continuing to roll on became apparent. There was no saying, "I just don't want to today." If life went on, then I best get on with it as well.

Also, I was raised with the Midwest work ethic. No matter how much you want something, wanting doesn't make it happen. Clear intention paired with hard work makes things happen.

With that as a backdrop I will tell you that there was a moment when simply taking life each day and in stride changed. The nature of my calling in life had been in a state of fluctuation for many years. Between resisting God's call, to attempting to answer what I felt was God's call, and then back to seeking again, it was a period when so many thoughts bounced around in my mind.

More than that, I had questions. What is it God wants from me? As much as I would have loved to have been a missionary, my body would not hold up to such work. I would have loved to travel the world, in service of God's kingdom and His people, to spread the good news of Jesus. That was just not going to happen.

How do I use the talents I have to serve God? Ordained ministry really was no longer an option. Seminary wasn't going to work. And yet God had given me gifts and talents that needed to be used. I've wondered where the Holy Spirit of God would lead me. Perhaps my calling would lead to another place and another role.

I was enjoying my work with the young people at Prince of Peace Lutheran Church. Teaching confirmation and Sunday school had renewed my heart following the nerve injury. Working with both the kids and the other adults on the team brought a sense of purpose back into my life.

Our confirmation kids were in junior high school, not an easy age. It's not easy for those in junior high, nor is it easy for those of us who choose to work with and love them. Yet the challenge of finding ways to reach them was delightful. The more I did, the more I wanted to do.

Adults were also a part of my experience at that time. It was during this time that the HAGS came together. While I was teaching children (especially their children) I was forming wonderful Christian friendships with their parents.

There were retreats and other special events that allowed my skills and talents to be used. Organizing and creating gave me an opportunity to use some skills from my regular workdays. As well, there were chances for me to continue to develop my skills at delivering God's message.

Life in those days was really beginning to feel full. I could speak of the lost dream of seminary without crying. There was anticipation and joy in the challenge to teach and make God's word practical and meaningful to everyone. This was important for those young people and sometimes even more so for adults. The same holds true to this day.

More than anything, in those days, I was experiencing contentment with my life in the church. The need to be in constant pursuit of any new way to serve or any new way to pursue ordination had been replaced by a joy in the moment that came from an ever-growing sense that I was living into God's calling. It may not look like I thought it would. Nevertheless, I was serving the God I loved and whom I knew loved me.

Things began to evolve from that point when other opportunities presented themselves. My longtime friend, Reverend Scott Maxwell-Doherty, called one day with an invitation for me to serve on the planning team for the ELCA's National Youth Gathering. I had attended several of those gatherings and even performed at one of them. I was ecstatic at the opportunity to be a part of another gathering and to work with my dear friend.

Scott and Melissa were serving a parish in Grand Forks, North Dakota. You have to believe in the calling of God's Holy Spirit when you move from Scottsdale, Arizona, to Grand Forks, North Dakota. It is not a thing a person does without the Spirit of God behind them. Scott had remained active in youth ministry and was known to the folks responsible for pulling together the program for the Y2K gathering. He told me our team leader was a pastor from Texas named Scot Sorensen. We would begin to tell the two Scot-tts apart by whether their name ended in one or two Ts.

Our initial meeting (January 1999) was in St. Louis, Missouri, the site of the gathering. It was a particularly frigid January when I flew to meet members of the team. I borrowed a down coat and layered, baby, layered.

Our team was tasked with planning the Bible study and related programming for the morning mass gatherings in the dome. Other teams would be in charge of evening programming, hotel life, transportation, security, and a myriad of other things necessary to make a gathering of this magnitude possible. Some of the members of those other teams were in St. Louis for this preliminary meeting as well.

Weather had delayed arrival of many of the flights. This meant that most of us would not meet until breakfast the following morning. I checked into the hotel, and was advised that my roommate (pre-assigned by the ELCA gathering staff) would be a late arrival. Other than Scott, I knew no one on the team. Okay, that made me a little anxious.

Shortly after midnight, my roommate arrived. Her name was Chloe. We hit it off instantly, yet little did I know how important she would be to my story. A couple of hours later, Chloe answered a knock at our door and, before I knew it, my old friend Scott was flying onto my bed and I was getting a bear hug. Scott and I began to laugh hysterically. Soon David and Chloe joined us on the bed and the laughter continued. It was a silly and delightful way to meet some new friends. Scott had arrived with David Hunstad. Scott, David, and Chloe all knew one another from the professional Youth Ministry Network. Now they were my friends as well.

Beginning with breakfast the following morning, our task was laid before us by the core planning group behind the event at ELCA church-wide. There was an educational component to this time. That core planning group had determined our theme and guiding scripture verses. We were introduced to scholars who attempted to give us background in all those scriptures in order that we might use that information in designing our portion of the program. The theme and the scripture would be incorporated into all aspects of the gathering. This first meeting of all the teams gave us time to learn a bit about St. Louis (World's Fair = first ice cream cone) and our way around our venue, the TWA Dome.

We were given time to meet in our teams. Our group bonded quickly and set about the task of creating a special experience for the church's young people. Around the table were youth lovers (some call them youth workers—I use the term youth lover—because as my mom always said, we do for love what we would not do for money) from across the country. People whose vocation is working with kids do it for the love of Jesus and His children.

The group was a delightful mix of ordained clergy, church professionals, and high school–aged folks. Those young people were there for their particularly important perspective on our work. How would we possibly create programming for high school–aged folks without having their input? To a one, each had experiences, talents, and interests that would make the creative task before us (daunting as it was) a most exciting adventure.

We would meet several times in the following eighteen months leading up to the gathering. Some of us would write scripts, others would work with the talent (speakers and musicians) we would use, and others would work on the logistics of our massive production. A few in our group had done similar things, but this production took all of us to a new level.

A subcommittee was formed from our group to plan the gatherings closing worship service. Worship is something I enjoy, so I volunteered. My friend Rev. Melissa Maxwell-Doherty was tagged to chair our subcommittee. To those who know and love her, she is referred to as the worship queen. Combine passion and talent as she has, and you get a well-deserved reputation.

Between S.L.A.M. (St. Louis A.M.) and the worship subcommittee, I did some considerable traveling. I was having a blast! My creativity was running free. And more than that, I was engaged in ministry. Here I was, doing something wonderful for the church. Perhaps people will come to understand the love of Jesus through the work we are doing. This was our regular prayer.

The realization that this work was just as much God's work as being a parish pastor came slowly to me. Clearly, God was at work in each of us as we wrote scripts and chose music to fit the moments we were creating. There were also the worship meetings, which included writing and/or reviewing litanies and prayers. Even the more mundane things like attempting to figure out how to commune 18,000 people in twelve minutes (it can be done) seemed filled with God's Spirit.

We came to our team meeting in November 1999 with the intention of making decisions about speakers, music, and the overall flow of the program. It was important to get our talent booked and allow our scriptwriters a format within which to work.

I also confess that I went to St. Louis remembering some of the wicked fun we had as a group at our previous meetings and in full and great expectation of more laughter. We had also been experiencing some tough times. Chloe had been battling cancer. She had been a bold and stalwart part of the group, but it was hard to miss the fact that she was fighting the good fight, yet not beating the disease. That November she seemed weaker, but she was there and as usual ready to do her amazing part in our creative process.

Over the year of working together we had developed bonds based on appreciation of our diverse personalities and styles. And there were characters in our group. Creative personalities were important, and boy did we have them. Trust me when I tell you they have "big personalities"—it is evident in the fact that I am not the most outrageous person at the table. And I mean this in the best possible way!

It was one of those groups of people I love to be around. We could and would laugh in one moment, cry and comfort one another in the next, and then be laser clear and direct about the work at hand.

We began our time together with an announcement. David Hunstad (who was at that time assistant to the bishop of the Northwest Minnesota Synod) had for months been throwing around the idea for a new business. David is a man of great humor and wit, and we had encouraged him to pursue his idea for a line of Lutheran identity wear. So before we got down to business, David passed out the first edition of his "Old Lutheran" T-shirts. The brand launched in the fall of 1999 is now David's primary business. Primarily web based (www.oldlutheran.com), Old Lutheran is now the "Official Center for Lutheran Pride—But Not Too Proud." I'm fond of bragging that I have one of those first-edition shirts.

This is just one example of the passion and creativity within our group.

It was now time to get to our primary agenda. This was the selection of some of the talent that we would use to communicate the message of each day. Our writers had been working on scripts for each day of the gathering centering them around the appointed theme and scripture text. Although there was much work yet to be done, we were at a decision point. Speakers needed to be selected, contacted, and contracted as soon as possible. Then, based on what the speakers would present, the scripts could be finished.

I was grateful to be working with folks who were so much more connected to the world of professional youth ministry than I. Preliminary discussion had been taking place among our team leaders Scot, Scott, and David. They would have ideas and know people who would be up to the task. I knew how to make a speech, but I did not know any of the folks who were doing this kind of work.

Choosing the right speaker seemed to me a critical task. So much of our program content was entrusted to our keynote speakers. Certainly music and other media were important. But whenever you give over seventeen-minute blocks of time it is essential to follow the wisdom of Yoda (from *Star Wars*): "Choose wisely." I was excited to hear the names our leaders were going to recommend. Having been on the script-writing group, I was also invested in the success of our speakers.

Our team leader Scot had a history of both working with youth and on events such as this. He is also a linear thinker, so we began our speaker discussion with our first day. Thematic review focused us on the need for a speaker who could convey the message of "welcome." We specifically wanted the message to be of God's great welcome to us all. Whether stranger or longtime member, God welcomes everyone. We are welcomed at his table of grace and more; we have a home in God's own heart. I got excited all over again, for the power of God's message to bring new perspective to the young people who would be participating in the gathering.

David began, "So for this day, we are unanimous in our recommendation. The person we think is perfectly suited to bring this message is—Paula Sturgeon."

"Who?" I said.

"You," he said.

I was stunned, amazed, delighted, honored, and more. There was no way that I could have anticipated his words. Certainly I had done some speaking, even keynote speaking, but never to an audience of tens of thousands, and never a speech of this importance.

As my mind swirled to grasp the enormity of the honor and challenge bestowed upon me, I recall having my peers on the team applauding. They were all so supportive and affirming that I found myself in the midst of an emotional high. Excited and delighted, I was also humbled.

Beyond humbled, I was clearly aware that I needed to pray before saying yes or no. Prayer would be critical for me to be effective in my communication and therefore the place where I needed to begin. And here was my prayer: "Let this be for your truth and your glory, Lord. When I tell my own story, help me to be clear that it is really Your story."

I had an additional need, that being to talk to Chloe. Chloe and I had an immediate affinity for one another that began at our first meeting. Her grace, humor, and courage in facing her cancer inspired me. We laughed together more than you could imagine any two broken-down bodies would. Chloe had been in our room resting. Her breathing had been labored and she was exhausted from the respiratory distress. She had not been in the room when the invitation was made and endorsed by the team. Consequently, I was anxious to tell her of the invitation, and more so, hear her feedback.

Chloe had been our group's mother hen, and I treasured her perspective on everything. She would be honest with me. If she felt it important to have a more professional speaker she would tell me so. And if she thought the young people would be better served by someone else, she wouldn't shield me from her truth. If Chloe endorsed me as a speaker it would mean so much.

Our team had taken a break, and I had gone immediately to our room to see her. I was grateful she was awake. Otherwise (truthfully), I might have been tempted to make noise in the hope she would awaken. *(Bratty, I know.)*

I began by checking on how she was feeling. Chloe and I had this sort of "wink wink" verbal dance. One would ask the other, "How are you doing?" The other would respond, "I'm fine." We knew all too well that each had physical considerations and that sometimes "fine" was as good as it would get. There was no need for details. I could hear her labored breathing and see her ashen skin color. She was well aware that my walking pace was slowed and I didn't stand as straight as I did on other occasions. We just knew and so there was no need to belabor the point.

"Tell me," she asked. "What have I missed?"

"Not much," I was about to burst. "Just the fact that they asked me to be the first morning's keynote speaker."

"Yeah!" she cheered. Chloe proceeded to tell me that she knew they were going to ask me. Of course she knew; Chloe was always in the know. I couldn't believe that I had not thought of that.

"So you think I am an okay choice?" As I write this I'm struck at how much I needed additional affirmation. It was ridiculous, bordering on being suckie! All the affirmation I needed was contained within the invitation. Plainly said, if they didn't think I was a good choice, they would not have extended the offer. Chloe had to believe that I was a good choice or she would have vetoed my name before the meeting.

My wise friend spent the next half hour giving me her wonderful counsel. She affirmed not only the invitation to be one of the gathering's keynote speakers, but went on to discuss my gifts, talents, and calling. In the year that we had known one another, she told me she had learned much about me. Yet she went on to say that she wanted to know more of my story and particularly she wanted to hear more about my faith journey with Jesus. Tell the story, she encouraged; tell the story of God's great love. Telling the story she said was my "true calling."

"True calling." Those were her exact words. They had a lyrical quality when she said them. "True calling" were also the words that I had wanted, even needed, to hear. The trauma of the last five years had left me wondering. Wondering about the nature of my calling in God's kingdom. After years of soul-searching, I had felt ready to step forward into a life in the ministry. Seminary followed by ordained ministry was my calling. And yet, that calling died on an operating room table.

Certainly I now felt useful and part of the work of God's people and, on occasion, I even felt called to the work I was doing with young people. I was happy doing what I was doing. It was enjoyable and worthwhile. But, and I'm almost ashamed to admit it, it did not fill that empty place in my heart. Was I selfish to want more? Well, perhaps. Call it whatever you wish, but I was still searching. Maybe Chloe said it best when she used the term "true calling." We all respond to a variety of callings in our lives; in our work life, home life, and relationships. And the way in which we respond to these callings brings meaning, a flavor and beauty to our lives. They can also bring pain, joy, purpose, puzzlement, and so much more.

"True calling" boils it all down to the essential. The essential reveals our essence. It defines us through the most important lens, which is through the graceful, loving eyes of God. Our true calling is that for which we have been created, gifted, and empowered. When we dwell in our true calling it is no longer our work that is seen, it is our worth. Our worth, defined solely through God's grace, as He calls us His children.

Chloe suggested this was the door through which I would come to understand God's true calling in my life. The ancient poet Boccaccio wrote: "They speak truth who breathe their words in pain." I felt sufficiently connected to Chloe's suffering to trust that she was speaking truth. She was not just being nice. Nice as she was, truth was her only gear. Her final admonition to me that afternoon was, "You will be great and the young people will be blessed."

Not surprisingly, my mother said nearly the same thing. She knew I could do it and shared with me the joy of being invited to something so special.

In the ensuing months leading up to the gathering, there was so much to be done. Scripts were formalized and other production details were addressed. And while I was excited about my speech it seemed a back-burner issue. There seemed to be time to prepare my speech later as other things seemed more pressing.

Actually, I think I was procrastinating. Oh, heck, I know I was. Avoiding the task meant avoiding my self-doubt. There is always that awful voice in the back of my mind that says, "Nobody wants to hear what you have to say," or "Who would find anything interesting in your life?" It is a wicked part of my psyche, and I'm betting I'm not the only person who must quiet that kind of negative self-talk from time to time.

Beyond self-doubt there was another hurdle to cross. I had to come to terms with the need to be authentic. In order to be effective as a speaker, I had to be willing to tell the truth of my life. And not just the joys or the moments of realizing God's love: I had to give voice to the struggles as well. My task was to paint a picture with words and that picture had to be complete. If I was to do this, I knew I needed to be as forthright as possible.

Knowing of the need to be open and authentic and actually doing so are two different things. The former is an intellectual exercise, which can be done behind closed doors, in the dark, with no one watching. It may be mentally tasking but no one need know. The latter is 180 degrees different. Authenticity exists only in the light. It is the public demonstration of our inward self. And more, authenticity requires one to be truthful—even when the truth doesn't appear to be pretty.

When I agreed to be one of the presenters, I had not given an ounce of thought or consideration to the internal struggle this would trigger. Preparations for the speech took me on an emotional journey to places I had avoided. Some of those places had been in my psyche's "out of bounds" for years. Therapeutic counseling (which I had done from time to time in my life and have been well served by) might well have been appropriate. This time, however, what I ended up doing is writing a speech. It proved to be a most therapeutic exercise. Laying out the story of my life, warts and all, allowed me to relive the hurts and begin the healing process. *(A seventeen-minute speech turned out to be a small practice run when compared with writing a book.)*

Our program team had designed unique ways to introduce each day's keynote speaker. Mine was to be a sort of pop-up video. Pop-ups had been popular additions to the music videos shown on MTV and VH-1. The pop-ups contained random pieces of information about the performers, the song, and/or the video itself.

My video introduction was a montage of pictures with biographical pop-ups set to a short piece of the song "Can't Last a Day" by the Contemporary Christian group Avalon. The pictures and text would give a basic and simple picture of my life. My job would be to tell my story without pictures.

The Gathering finally arrived. Our team moved into a great hotel adjacent to the TWA Dome in St. Louis. In just a couple of days twenty thousand young people and those who love them would descend upon the city. They would come into the dome ready to be moved by God's Holy Spirit. They came to sing and to dance at the crossroads of our country and at the crossroads of their lives. Our team stood inside the massive venue and was awed by the size of the space and the enormity of the responsibility before us.

Immediately we began our work of preparing staging and putting the final touches on our program and script. I had been part of the writing group and therefore worked with the young, talented people who would be our emcees. In the previous eighteen months, I had learned more than I could have dreamed about live productions, and now it was time to put all of that into action.

Our leaders met with the dome's production professionals to review our daily run sheets. These were the detailed agendas for each day and included the order of music, performers, and speakers. The production team would cue the musicians and play videos as per our direction. A member of our team would remain backstage with the performers and speakers and cue them to the stage following that same run sheet. I would share this role with Scott.

Wednesday afternoon was sound check time for those who were to be on stage that evening for the opening program, and for those who were to be on stage the following morning. This included me. I was fit for a wireless microphone and told to speak portions of my speech so that the sound guy could set the appropriate levels for my microphone and the audio feed.

Oh crap! I had been working diligently to memorize my speech, but suddenly I felt at a loss to know where to begin. This was really happening and now my anxiety level was skyrocketing. While the technical folks were getting some details resolved, I prayed. My prayer was more for a calm heart. "Lord, you have brought me this far, help me to get the job done."

When I got the cue from the stage manager, I began at the beginning. And it felt great, easy, and right. I was my father's child and he loved the spotlight. And now I knew I was falling in love with it myself.

Staging and details were next. The plan was for me to enter stage left on an electric scooter. I would head across to center stage, turn, and face the audience. The audio guys in the booth would bring up my microphone as I made the turn at center stage so that I could begin speaking from the scooter. When the speech was over, I would get back on the scooter and drive away.

According to the run sheet, there would be a video and then a song from our musical director Ken Medema (a most gifted and talented musician) and the house band before my introductory video. I would move from the "green room" backstage into position to go up the two ramps leading to the stage as Ken and the band finished their song. When my video began, I was to make my way up the side ramps to be ready to cross the stage at the conclusion of the video. The plan was perfect.

Beware of perfect plans. I sat backstage Thursday morning with Scott and watched as each piece of the run sheet was completed. I was nervous but not overly so. It helped that I was sitting there with my good friend Scott. I had spent time in prayer and now was calmly ready to make my presentation. We even laughed, but it was easy to be calm when there was still ten minutes to go. There was a video and then Ken and the house band and then I would take the stage. Nice and easy.

The video began to play when both Scott and I came to a startling realization. It was the wrong video. It was my pop-up video introduction being played too soon. Oh my God! I had forty-five seconds to be on stage. Cripples like me don't move fast, even on a scooter.

My adrenaline level shot through the roof. Scott and I quickly scrambled to get from backstage and up the two ramps so that I would be ready to be on stage at the end of my introductory video. My heart was pounding. I was so anxious to make my queue and hit my mark that everything else seemed a blur.

I made it up the two ramps just as the video was concluding and proceeded to head onto the stage as planned. Blame it on adrenaline or on my single focus of getting to my mark, but I drove the scooter onto the stage at way too high a speed. I was going too fast to make the left turn that I needed to make to face the audience at center stage. I did not realize I was going too fast until I turned left and nearly laid the scooter over.

I made the turn on two wheels and nearly fell onto the stage. My thoughts moved at a lightning pace. First, dear God, don't let me fall. Then: if I do fall, how am I going to get up, and most importantly, remember your microphone is live so don't curse out loud. Thankfully I was able to keep the "Oh shit!" inside. This all took place in nanoseconds and included my final plan: if you fall, simply toss it back to Ken and ask for assistance getting up.

All that panic was for naught. By the grace of God the scooter stayed upright. The teenagers in the audience went crazy. They thought it was a planned stunt. Clearly they did not hear the quiver in my voice during the first five minutes of my speech. It was the remnants of the adrenaline rush.

Having come through such a challenging beginning, the remainder of the speech went very well. There is a point in my talk that I shared with those young people my frustration with God following the nerve injury in my arm. I told them there were days when I screamed "Why me?" I screamed those words in the dome as I shared that part of the story. Sometimes that technique can seem absurd or phony to an audience. Yet those young people moved with me to journey from those moments of screaming to the times of silence and heartbreak that followed. I assured them that there is space in our relationship with Jesus for both our pain and our joy. Jesus is present when we scream and when we sing.

There was more to share with them. It was fun to invite them to laugh with me even at times when laughter seemed the furthest thing from my mind. My speech concluded with an invitation for all of them to be keenly aware of God's open heart and invitation to journey with us.

A little bumper sticker theology would be my final piece before I climbed onto the scooter to exit the stage. I had first seen this bumper sticker on the back of a Corvette. It read: Get in—Sit down—Shut up—and Hang on! How do you make that into a faithful statement you ask? Well, it's easy. It goes like this:

- Get in—get into a relationship with God—take the first step…
- Sit down—Relax and give it some time—don't be so anxious to do the next thing on your agenda…
- Shut Up—Listen—through prayer we make known to God what is on our hearts but spend an equal or greater time in quiet; listen for His leading…
- Hang on—You are about to go on the ride

of your life, for where the Spirit of God takes
you, that is where you need to be…

With that and more than a little trepidation, I climbed onto the scooter and drove off stage. I was pretty anxious about that last drive. So anxious that I failed to realize the tremendous applause I was receiving. There was a standing ovation.

Making my way through the crowd to the place where my mother was seated was my first priority. I needed to see her face and hear her thoughts. When I got to my mother, she had tears in her eyes. She put her arms around me and held me. She told me she loved me. It was all the affirmation I needed.

For the remaining days of the gathering, wherever I went in and around the venue, I was warmly greeted by young people and adults. Some even asked for my autograph. I would respond, "I'm happy to give you my autograph, but I am no rock star." One young man replied, "Heck yeah, you are a rock star, to me." Perhaps that's why I was there.

In those days, the entire gathering production was replayed a second week. The number of people who wanted to attend the gathering made it impossible to find a suitable venue that would hold them all. We, in essence, did our show twice. The first week there were a little more than twenty thousand attendees, and in the second week just a little fewer. Our teams had Monday and Tuesday to rest and recuperate before the second week began on Wednesday.

We met with the production team from the Dome

to review notes. I wanted to make sure that the video cues were in proper order. I don't think my heart could have stood a second week like the first. Not to worry, all went well. Everything that second week went just as planned.

After I gave my speech the second time I was chatting with some of the folks from the security team. They told me they were disappointed that I did not do my wheelie trick as I came on stage. I told them that was no trick, rather a moment of extreme panic saved by the grace of God. They honestly thought that I had been able to do that on purpose. Oh Lord!

Chloe was right, this was my "true calling." Making that speech had been a joy and a blessing. Living the life that led up to and was contained within that speech had not seemed like such a blessing. But it was in that two-week period of telling my story that I realized how God had been at work all along. My life was His gift to me. My gift to Him would be sharing my life with others for His glory. No need for false humility. I was not telling my story, I was telling God's story. It has been my "true calling" ever since.

Today, Chloe lives among the saints in light and in the hearts of those who loved her and were blessed to know her. She gave me a gift I shall always treasure—an invitation to my "true calling."

The experience at the ELCA National Youth Gathering was the "tipping point" for the next phase of my life work in God's church.

I had been well received *(no brag—just fact)* and consequently been blessed by many additional invitations to speak to a variety of groups across the country. My moment in the spotlight led to more opportunities to tell God's story.

Since that summer of 2000, I have claimed as my "true calling" the role of itinerant storyteller and evangelist. Traveling from north to south, east to west, I tell the story of God's great love for us all as I have experienced it through my own life. Over the years, my story has grown and evolved. This happens to everyone. Life experiences and time have their inevitable impact. Yet through it all there remains the great constant—the abiding love of God as we have received it through Jesus the Christ. My story has new chapters, which continue to be blessed and elevated by "the old, old story of Jesus and His love."

My travels have taken me many places. I rarely travel alone because of the fatigue factor and the toll it takes on my body. The time spent with my traveling companions has always been a wonderful additional blessing. In the beginning, my mother was my primary travel partner. She was great and we had good times together. And, since she has been my caregiver for so many years, we have great ease with one another. But the physical demands of it all leave us exhausted when we return home. Consequently, we have chosen (with some exceptions) for Mother to stay at home and nurse me back to health when I return from the road. It's a plan that works well for both of us.

My niece Callie was the first to travel with me. In August 2001, we went to New York for an ELCA

Regional Youth Gathering. The event was held at Wagner College on Staten Island. I was excited to share the trip with Callie because there would be opportunities for us to see some sites in addition to the time spent doing our work. Callie has an artistic talent and the chance to take her to the Metropolitan Museum of Art was thrilling.

Callie is my sister Julie's daughter. She has always been a strong and delightful child and in many respects mature beyond her years. Although this trip took place just before her tenth birthday she was quite capable and up to the task. Her caring nature made her a great companion for me, as she was willing to tie shoes, pull luggage, or whatever else it took to be of assistance.

I loved being able to spend time with her. We had some interesting experiences along the way. Despite being short on time and my limited mobility, we crammed a good bit into our trip. We rode the Staten Island Ferry back and forth to Manhattan, took the Liberty and Ellis Island tours, spent an afternoon at the Metropolitan Museum of Art, and even ventured into Times Square.

We stayed in one of the dormitories at the college, which meant no television in our room. That left us with the opportunity to talk, laugh, and just plain giggle over the silliness we casually observed throughout our day. At night we wore our pajamas to the lobby and bought ice cream from the vending machines. Being Aunt Paula meant not worrying about a balanced diet.

During one of our ferry rides into Manhattan, a stranger suggested we stand at a certain spot that would give us a special view of the twin towers of the World Trade Center. The optical illusion made it appear that the buildings grew as we got closer to the lower

Manhattan dock. It was most impressive stuff to a child. The power of that moment came home to me just one month later on September 11, 2001. As I sat in horror watching those buildings fall, I prayed for the people of New York, feeling a kinship with them from our short time spent there. I also gave a prayer of thanksgiving to God that Callie had the opportunity to see the towers. When we spoke after she finished school that day, she wondered if she was among the last people to see the buildings standing. Her innocent outlook was thankfully still intact.

Callie's memories from that trip aren't as complete as I would have wished. I suppose there is a selfish part of me that wishes she remembered (and certainly fondly) her trip to New York with Aunt Paula. And maybe that's a pretty universal human thing. But I have come to realize that it is our own memories that we must treasure. We have no control over how things do or do not remain with others. Memories matter to the individual who holds them. So, New York is a treasure to me for time spent with my Callie. She has since graduated from high school and headed to college. I recognize that she is growing up, but a part of her will always be ten years old and traveling with me.

My travels have left me great memories of wonderful places and delightful people. From the people responsible for inviting me, to those who take the time to chat with me after I speak, they have left me with so many treasured memories.

This calling from God has taken me from the frozen

north to the sunshine of Texas. Yes, I have accepted invitations to speak in subzero North Dakota and Minnesota. *(Layering is critical.)* Through these trips I have made connections with some of the great members of the kingdom of God. They are responding to Jesus' Great Commission to make disciples by working with young people and the adults who love them. This means sleeping (hardly) on gymnasium floors, pulling all-nighters on buses, eating things (well, let's don't go there), all in the name of being in a relationship with young people for the sake of Jesus. They lead mission trips to places ravaged by the forces of nature or captive to the grip of poverty. Creature comforts are never part of the package.

In my book, these are the rock stars!

God works through others to work His will in our lives. I was blessed by Chloe's influence in my life. Others have equally blessed me as well. God has placed me in the company of so many remarkable people, and I count each experience a treasure.

Now, there are also times when I have been around people with whom I am, shall we say, less than excited. We have all had some tough relationships in our lives. I'm not talking about strictly those who are brutal or difficult in the extreme. I've had relationships with people who are challenging to my values, who do not share my priorities, or who can be a general pain in the butt. Yet even in those relationships I have learned not only about myself but also about the nature of God.

If grace is truly the free and wholly unmerited

gift of God then it is given to all, even those whom I dislike or find disagreeable. God's grace-full love of the disagreeable helped me realize God's grace-full love for me. Grace is God's action; God's choice to love us all. God's choice to love us as demonstrated by our Savior Jesus Christ.

Good and gracious God,
Lord of my heart's true calling,

Seek me and search me,
awaken me and empower me,
guide me and mold me,
and reveal to me,
through people and experiences,
the true nature of my calling as a child of God.

Amen

13

When Gimpy Gets Gloomy

Yea, though I walk through the valley of the shadow of death, I will fear no evil: for thou art with me; thy rod and thy staff they comfort me.

—Psalm 23:4 (KJV)

Everybody gets the blues sometime.
There's no exception to the rule.

I am an extrovert. I like to be around people, and garner energy in so doing. Nothing winds me up like the chance to be at a conference and meet new people and see old friends. I have been known to go longer and stronger in the hallways of such gatherings than when I'm at the podium making a speech.

When speaking, I love large crowds for the energy they bring. Once you get a crowd rolling with you, as a speaker or when preaching, the work becomes much easier. Energy builds upon energy. There have been moments for me when I have felt an almost out-of-body experience. This is when the joy of sharing the Good News of God's gracious love is so personally overwhelming that I have the clear feeling of the presence of the Holy Spirit. Nothing compares to the sense that you are completely one with God. It is awesome!

And yet, there is something powerful, and often profoundly so, that occurs in a smaller group. It is a wondrous thing to share my story and see it resonate on the faces of the people in the audience. They are, in some manner, having a personal experience of grace. In witnessing my faith, I pray that people are given an example of living grace. To bring the love of God in Jesus to people in this manner is a privilege. And it never gets old nor ceases to amaze me.

I also love the question and answer opportunities that occur more readily in small groups. There are a few standard questions about my health. Some kind folks ask if I have written a book. Thank the Lord, I now have a better answer than "I'm working on it."

Here's my reality check. Although I love my work and feel truly called by God to do His work, it is often exhausting.

You may be saying, "Of course work is exhausting. What do you expect?" I'd answer that you are right. Work can, and perhaps sometimes should, be exhausting. I'm reminded of a sign I once saw: "It ain't easy being the queen."

Really, I am not complaining. I actually love to be physically tired. I love the feeling of having done something and afterwards feeling spent. Recently I have enjoyed planting flowers. The beauty of nature, digging in the dirt, and feeling the sunshine on my body is all so good. Afterwards I'm tired. And I love it. Work that tires the body is, I believe, good for the soul.

This is different from how I feel following my speaking, preaching, and other evangelical work. This work leaves me physically tired but, more than that, emotionally exhausted. I pour myself into the work. My presentations are never written and, I truly believe, come from the Lord. Thus I'm a vessel for the Word to be proclaimed. By the grace of God the work—His work—gets done.

When I finish a speech I am ready for a quiet place to gather my thoughts and my energy. Generally this works out, but not always. The older I get, the less bounce-back I have. *(Don't panic!—I'm sure that it's just me!)* There are also occasions when the recovery time takes several days.

It is in those times of emotional, physical, or spiritual exhaustion that the blues creep into my life. Just as in battle, when your soldiers are tired, the foe takes advantage. The foe (the blues) is more correctly called depression. It's an overly analytical and introspective process that strips away my self-confidence and throws my life's gear into a halting neutral and I lose interest.

On my list of things about which I plan to speak to the Lord (on the occasion of our face-to-face meeting— or perhaps it would be better form to wait until our second meeting) is this question: why, when our bodies and spirits are so tired and low, do our personal doubts and fears appear to have such strength and resilience? Why, oh why, do I have the energy for self-pity and despair when I don't have enough for lightness, let alone joy?

You will not hear me using the "devil made me do it" argument. I want to be clear that I believe there is evil in our world, and that there is a darkness in any heart given the right circumstances. But I do not personally subscribe to the notion that the devil moves into our specific situations to manipulate them for dark purposes.

On this point, if need be, I hope we may agree to disagree.

My thoughts are more inclined toward casting accountability at our own human condition. In the moments when life is tough, we either stew in it or rise to the occasion. Often we do some of both. We are all, to some degree, susceptible to the gravitational pull of our own inner darkness. And when that happens, it can take significant effort to tread water fast enough to rise to or remain above the surface.

When we ruminate upon an issue, we are stuck in a first-person bog, where all we can see is ourselves. Rarely, if ever, have I passed a mirror without checking myself. But metaphorically to stand and stare at the reflection would be not only boring but counterproductive in the extreme. Yet I can tell you that I have been there, done that. Whether preceded by exhaustion or not, I have fallen under the grasp of my own self-interest. Well, even that is a self-serving and yet not wholly accurate phrase. Better to say my negative self takes over. And truthfully there really is no interest served. Except perhaps to remove myself from life, which is really a poor way to rest and recuperate.

When I get the blues and feel depressed, I tend to ask rhetorical questions like "why didn't I" or chastise myself with the notorious "you should have…" and in that moment my emotional rat climbs on the running wheel. And once it has momentum, watch out. The rat only stops when there isn't anything left to spend.

I can find myself in emotional turmoil as well when I lament "what might have been." It would be a lie for me to tell you that I haven't been saddened by the absence of a husband and children. It can be a lonely time when, at the end of the day, there is no one lying next to you to hold you. Not that a husband is always the answer, but the companionship and warm embrace *(no feet—please)* would be welcomed.

Pain is also a precursor to depression for me. More specifically, the limitation of movement that comes from pain can bring me down. Generally and thankfully these depressive episodes are relatively rare. The amputation of my leg has brought some emotional challenges as well. I miss standing and walking with a sort of relative ease. I long to walk on the beach. Then my family reminds me that I haven't walked with ease for years and that we live in beach-less Arizona. Their perspective is most helpful.

And there is the issue of weight. This has been a constant challenge to me. I have always thought I was fat—even when I was at a more "normal" weight. Losing weight is tough for me, especially now that I live primarily in a chair. And when my weight becomes a focal point for me, the blues lurk in the center of my thought process. Pushing the food foes aside can only happen when I focus on the good stuff in my life. And I'm not referring to salty snacks.

Having said all that, I must tell you I do not have the "Why me?s." Perhaps with the exception of when I have a head cold (which is a huge bummer to me), I do not lament my circumstance. "Why Me?" is a question with only one answer. That answer being, "Why not me?" We all live under the human condition. Last I looked, nobody gets a pass; we all have life to live.

Clearly some have a tougher road than others. There are diseases and injuries that are far more challenging than mine. Not to forget the millions of children trying to grow up without families, homes, or sufficient food. Dr. Henri Nouwen wrote in his wonderful book, *Can You Drink the Cup?* about the joys and sorrows of life. His admonition that our own sorrows gain perspective when we look as well at the sorrow of the world and that of Christ crucified. Dr. Nouwen's book should be on every reading list.

Those who appear to have easier paths are no more blessed than the others are cursed. It isn't about the Chosen doing better because God has blessed them. Nor is it that those with challenges have them because they have been cursed. Jesus died for us all, and through Him we are able to experience joy with sorrow. Our cup of life contains both. It is our shared human struggle that we must examine and understand. The pain and the joy.

I am blessed to have a family who has loved and stuck with me. Beyond that, I am blessed and thankful for God who is with me through it all. A God who says, "I know pain and I know you. My faith is in *you*."

Even happy people get the blues. This is because happy people are people. Emotional highs and lows are part of our humanity. It is part of what makes us unique, and emotional reaction to people and circumstances is different for everyone.

As I preach of my life in the Lord, I do so with a heart that has known both sorrow and joy firsthand. And in so doing I have found value in every moment, because I am keenly aware of Christ's presence in them all. Recognizing that there is no laughter without tears has been important for me. I love to laugh and so I must accept that the tears may come.

Comedy, as the Greeks knew all so well, is rooted

in tragedy. We cannot discern the difference between comedy and tragedy without the experience of both. Our highs are what they are only when seen through the perspective of our lows. Granted, this may be hard to grasp in the midst of tough times, but it is the truth. We know from Scripture (John 8:32) that *"the truth will set you free."* In fact, it is the only thing that can.

We all have some sort of traps or triggers in our psyches, pitfalls that can derail our moods, if not our entire lives. Avoiding them is always our first option. Nobody wants to accidentally fall into an emotional trap or trip any kind of trigger that might adversely impact our life. Consequently, we attempt to be diligent in maneuvering around them. Even that aversion to emotional traps or triggers can lead us into such risk avoidance that our lives become emotionally closed down. No risk—no reward.

What are your trips and/or triggers? I have shared that my blues can come with fatigue, pain, or any discussion of my weight. I'm not always able to avoid my triggers. Truthfully, none of us can always avoid the emotional issues that come from/with living life. Perhaps our energy would be better spent finding the people and resources that can help and support us in/through our tough times.

Awareness is only one part of the story. When the inevitable occurs and you find yourself in the sticky place called emotional turmoil, what do you do? For what do you seek, grasp, and pull on in order to reach a position of emotional health and stability?

What does your support system look like? Do you have the resources needed to meet your own challenges?

We do not need to, nor should we, face the tough times alone. Whether it is professional counseling and/or medications, both of which have helped me, or a good friend, or our faith in God, it's important to know that we do not face anything well when we face it alone.

Good and gracious God,
Jesus—lover of my soul,
A simple prayer for the complexities of life,
Let me praise You when joy fills my heart,
and lean on You when sorrow is all I see.
Your grace is sufficient for me.
Thanks be to God!
Amen

14

A Fool and Her Leg Are Soon Parted

A cheerful heart is good medicine,
but a crushed spirit dries up the bones.

—Proverbs 17:22

Somehow, in the back of my mind, I knew the day could come. I had hoped and prayed that it would not, but I knew it was a possibility. Call it natural knowing; that sense you have of your own body and just exactly how it will or won't go.

Ten years earlier, I had agreed to what was represented as the surgery to end all surgeries on my right knee. Then, just as it was from childhood, my right knee was the source of consternation. My third total knee replacement was showing signs of instability and perhaps even infection. The range of motion was minimal at best.

Being under the care if a new surgeon means taking time to establish rapport and trust. Generally, surgeons are slow to warm to patients, especially chatty, challenging ones like me. But Dr. McLaren was a different breed of cat. He was gentle, articulate, and had a marvelous dry wit. I liked him almost instantly, mostly because he made me laugh. He was serious, but not lethally so.

In plain language and calm demeanor, he strongly recommended that I have the total knee replacement removed. He would then install an internal fixation apparatus. In other words, he would place a titanium rod up the femur and down the tibia and secure it with screws. In order to get this single piece of metal into my leg, he would remove the joint and seed the area with cadaver bone, which would grow and knit together with my own bone. My leg would no longer bend at the knee but it would be strong as steel—literally. And provide me with much needed stability.

Such a drastic procedure became a good thing when the likelihood that it would mean no more procedures on that leg was discussed. There were no certainties, but it was far more probable than the repeated knee replacements I would otherwise face.

Engineering the fixation apparatus was not easy. There were measurements and a variety of radiographic and nuclear medicine studies to be done in advance. My insurance company nearly had a stroke at the cost, yet was persuaded, like I was, by Dr. McLaren's reasoning.

The surgery brought with it a painful recovery. You don't cut and drill into bone without there being pain. Meds helped, but didn't fully cover the pain. Pain doesn't go away with narcotics; rather, you are simply able to either sleep through it or cope with it. The pain doesn't go away but, to an extent, your care about the pain does.

What really helped me get through it all was saying, "This is it." I even cried to my hospital team (my mom and Aunt Carol), "Tell me I don't have to go through this ever again. No more, please." They were so supportive and encouraging.

Days became weeks, weeks became months, and I

recovered and learned to walk (once again) on a fused leg. That leg had been fused when I was a child, so I had some old muscle memory working for me. It really isn't as difficult as you might think. Sometimes it's a pain in the rear (and everywhere else), but…I got by.

But now I was at yet another surgeon's office with problems in my right leg. Dr. McLaren was no longer operating because of a nerve problem in his own arm. Dr. Croft was very different—extroverted and chatty. His style was personal and he acted much more like a family practice doctor than a surgeon. He fixed broken bones and did joint replacements. The fixator apparatus was mechanically fascinating to him.

He had read Dr. McLaren's notes and reviewed my new battery of x-rays. When I pinpointed the pain it appeared to emanate from the area where one of the bolts was through the tibia. Dr. Croft offered the option of removing that bolt. I knew (from Dr. McLaren) that could be a possibility. Could it really be that simple? A quick outpatient procedure, remove the loose screw *(stop laughing)*, and off I go.

Waking up in the recovery room of this small outpatient surgery center seemed like every other time. At least it did until they brought my mother back to see me. She had that serious look on her face when she told me that it was apparent (using the surgical fluoroscope) that the rod was no longer securely fixed in the bone. The pain was not from the bolt. The entire apparatus had somehow not completely seeded within the bone and was now loose. My surgery-to-end-all-surgery had not.

At my follow-up appointment Dr. Croft suggested

that I see one of the doctors locally who specialized in bone loss. They would have more answers and options for me.

Now I could write a book about the challenge of finding a doctor who was willing to see me. This is a part of medicine that most people don't see. Some doctors have staff that are part Doberman Pinscher and are able to keep the "less desirable" cases off the doctors' agenda. No less than five relatively prominent surgeons in the area declined to see me.

With the help of friends who made calls on my behalf, I was finally able to be seen at the Mayo Clinic by Dr. Christopher Beauchamp. Dr. Beauchamp is not only the chair of the Department of Orthopedics, his interests in orthopedics includes failed joint replacements. He was actually Dr. Croft's first choice.

For all the formality of the Mayo Clinic and the prestige in which his colleagues hold him, I found Dr. Beauchamp to be the most genuine of men. He was steady, kind, and thorough. His humor always came with a twinkle in his eye.

Once again I went through the radiographic studies needed for him to make a full assessment.

Today was the day we were to hear his evaluation and recommendation. My mother and I have waited for doctors for much of my life. This time our anxiety was running pretty high and yet I was also pretty calm, the calm of being divorced from what's going on and almost watching yourself as though in a movie.

Dr. Beauchamp entered the room with his characteristic handshake (firm yet gentle) and came right to the point. Indeed, the rod was loose and was the cause of the breathtakingly sharp pain I experienced when I stepped just so.

He began, "We have, in my estimation, two options." Good. Options are good.

First, he offered to add some additional hardware, plates and such, to internally reinforce the bone. He cautioned that it would take some time to know if this would work and if the bone would even accept it. He also added (in what I have since grown to appreciate as his usual candor) that it was a painful procedure but he would do his best to help me manage the pain.

As I hear this, I thought, *More pain, oh no. I'm already living on twice a day long-acting morphine. Much more pain and the dose will be so high that I won't be functional.*

I came quickly back to focus when I heard him say option two. Good—here comes another one—I love options.

His voice was clear and direct when he said, "We would amputate your leg, above the knee, and help you learn to walk on a prosthetic limb."

Okay—now option three—you gotta have another option. I wanted to yell, "Please, another option, oh please another!" None came.

"Amputate" is such a sterile word. "Cut off" is a more vivid description. No matter what word you use, it is not a discussion you want to have. But as I said, it had been in the back of my mind, all along. Once my knee space was removed there was no more putting anything back in there.

I didn't cry in that moment. I took the news like the tough girl I was raised to be. Hear it all and then go home to react and decide. This had been our plan and I was sticking with it.

It helped that Dr. Beauchamp recommended that we not decide then and there. I felt connected to him in the moment when he suggested that we "go home, think about it, pray about it, and then get back to me." He also said that he would do likewise.

Leaving the office that day, I was numb. Overwhelmed by hearing the words. They were words I expected. Yet, in the hearing, they had taken on the power of reality.

Pray about it was exactly the right answer. At times of stress like these, it is best to let the doctors do the doctoring and place your faith in the One who has brought you safely thus far. It was imperative for me to let God do what only God can.

I had to make the decision, not my family. I needed their support for certain. But it had to be my decision. Both in the making of the decision, and in the living with the decision, I needed that peace of mind and spirit that can only come from above. This was not the time for gut-wrenching, hunker-down, buck-up, "I can do this" self-talk. Quite the contrary. God's Holy Spirit would bring me the peace that passes understanding. Resting in that peace would be critical for both my emotional and physical recovery.

There is a complete surrender that must occur: surrender to the reality that the limb will be gone and won't ever (this side of heaven) return. No matter how much I might regret the decision afterwards, it wasn't going to change the reality. To surrender to reality is perhaps the single most important factor in long-term happiness. As my old friend and teacher, David, would say: "What's so—So what—What now?"

When I felt ready, I first shared my decision with my mother. She and I cried as I said, and we heard, the words out loud. "I'm going to be an amputee," I said. So many of my previous health struggles had involved resisting and fighting back the ravages of the disease. This was different. This was surrender and acceptance. Therefore, in the midst of our tears was real serenity.

"Yes, and you will be all right," she replied. That's my mama!

Then came my explanation. I knew she didn't need to hear it, as she trusted and supported my decisions on my health. I needed to tell her and again, hear it out loud for myself.

It sounded something like this: The procedure to add new hardware comes with some real pain. It doesn't thrill me but I'm not letting fear of pain be my determining factor. The additional hardware would take several months to heal and perhaps more time to know if it will even work. If it is successful, there is no guarantee that it will hold for the remainder of my life. Whether or not it is successful, we still haven't removed amputation as a possibility in the future.

I chose amputation and a prosthetic limb as an affirmative move. *Let's do this now*, I thought, *while Mama is still healthy enough to care for me. Let's do this while my hospital team (Mama and Aunt Carol) is still available. And let's do this while I'm still young enough and hopefully strong enough to adapt to the prosthesis.*

This was my decision and now I needed to attend to a perhaps much tougher matter. REGRET. I have done things in the past that I have regretted. Regret can be overwhelming in that it tends to bring along its cohorts to your regret-based pity party. Regret rarely appears alone as a one-dimensional wish you had not done whatever. Regret is like a rock star who travels with an entourage. It brings with it guilt, shame, and self-doubt. These uninvited guests make regret more powerful and difficult to abandon. And they weave themselves into all our emotions and arenas of life. We can't simply regret a decision or action without at least the risk of a more pervasive emotional crisis.

The pain of regret and all its companions has been tough for me to shake in the past. I was absolutely clear that I would not subject myself to it again. When the decision was made, I was determined not to look backwards.

Having made the decision, I called Mayo, met once again with Dr. Beauchamp, and began the two-month-long wait for my place on his schedule. I didn't want to wait, but this man is just that busy. Besides, many of his patients have cancer and deserve more rapid action than I.

Two months passed quickly but not uneventfully. I began to tell friends and colleagues of my impending surgery. I'm not sure how I expected them to respond, but almost to a person their first comment was, "Oh no." I tried to explain and even though they remained sad they were also resolute in their support of me. Although I am blessed to have such friends, the "Oh no" began to take its toll on me. Emotionally, it was becoming harder and harder. I felt burdened by their reactions. There was that voice in my head shouting, "Hey people—it's not your leg they are cutting off—it's mine—pull it together!"

I have a tendency to shift into a supporting mode

when people around me are struggling. Compassion for people in difficult times comes to me readily. If I am being completely honest, I must admit that in those days I resented those who needed my support. Damn it, it was my turn to be supported. Eventually, I stopped telling people about the impending surgery. Information was shared on a need-to-know basis.

This is a wonderful example of how emotions can overtake us in tough times. When knee-deep in the hoopla, clarity is rarely present. And, in the midst of all that, guess who starts to dance around the edges of my consciousness? You guessed it—regret. The doubts were there. Had I really thought things through? Did I make a reasoned or an emotional decision? Doubts about the plan were even starting to frighten me. As fiercely as regret was trying to take a vocal position I also knew the way to defeat it. Or at least I prayed that my plan would work.

I would convene a sort of council to assist me in the determination. This would be my mother, Aunt Carol, and sister Julie. Three women, who loved me, always had my back, and were my support system. Honestly, they were also the ones who would be on the front lines now and into the future. Much of the care and assistance I would need would come from them. Their perspective and counsel was important in order for me to feel settled about the decision.

I knew that each would bring a unique perspective. Aunt Carol had spent her life working in the law. I felt she could/would be a sort of judge ensuring that all sides of the issue were presented clearly. She had sufficient medical background and in fact had worked with amputation patients through the legal practice with which she had been affiliated. Of paramount value was that she is a strong Christian woman who shared my faith in the Lord. She would help make sure that I didn't lose sight of that fact.

My sister Julie has strong analytical skills, which I needed for looking at such an emotional issue. She would keep me grounded and that would, in turn, bring me assurance that I hadn't been too much of an over-the-top optimist. Julie was newer on the faith journey, but she had respect for my faith and encouraged me to rest in my faith.

Mother's role wasn't clear to me beforehand. I didn't have a specific role I wished her to play. She had been there every other time, and I wasn't about to stop now.

When the Holy Spirit of God leads you somewhere or brings forth an idea, it's important to get onboard. I can tell you, from personal experience, that some of the best things in my life have come from the Spirit's leading.

Such was the case for my "Council of Women." Carol, Julie, Mother, and I gathered in our living room on a Sunday afternoon. They knew what they were there for and so I got us started with some opening comments. I wanted to convey my love and appreciation for each of them. And I shared my angst over whether or not I had made a reasoned decision. My fear of regret was overwhelming my fear of the surgery. "Help me," I pleaded.

Their roles in the ensuing two hours played out much like I had thought, although not completely. Julie asked most of the questions. She was direct and to the point and really made me think. Her talent for analysis proved invaluable.

Carol listened and used her skill to help me weigh the pros and cons. She was able to help me capture definite ways in which my faith would serve to carry me through this next phase in my life.

Both Julie and Carol affirmed my personal strength and the ability to meet any challenge. They also said that when all is said and done it was still my decision to make. And that they would support me any way I chose.

My sweet mother sat next to me and held and/or patted my hand. She didn't weigh in except in concurrence with Julie and Carol's comments of my strength and their promised support.

In those two hours, my emotional state went from fearful to faithful, from anxiety-ridden to anxious to get on with it. And I was filled with gratitude and love for three very special women. They blessed me that day and continue to do so every day.

My decision was set. I would have the amputation and do whatever it took to learn to walk again with a prosthesis. I felt, in a word, delighted!

Later that same day, I told my mother of another decision. Weary of people's sad faces, I wanted to put **my** mark on this process. A party seemed the answer. Timing could not have been better for the kind of party I wanted.

April 5, 2007, was the date scheduled for surgery. The Sunday before was April 1, 2007. Perfect! I sent invitations to friends with this text:

> A fool and her leg are soon parted.
>
> Please come kick up your heels with me while I still have two.

B.Y.O.B. and Potluck (please bring your favorite anything)

It was a wonderful party. We laughed and laughed. The HAGS even did their traditional "Dancing Queen." Some would call it dancing; others might say it's more of an exercise in group silliness. People brought chicken legs, leg-sana, and all kinds of great food. It was exactly what I needed heading into the pre-op falderal and surgery. I think it also helped my friends; seeing my head up, facing the future cheerfully and faithfully.

Some who weren't able to be there sent me messages and cards. A clergy friend, noting that the surgery was on Maundy Thursday, suggested that I was in for a "heck of a foot washing." I loved that!

I had also joked with a friend who had retired from the Mayo Clinic Foundation that I "always knew it would cost me an arm and a leg to go to the Mayo Clinic and that I had hoped they would settle for just a leg." Lance gave me a mocked-up invoice from Mayo. It read:

SURGERY	*1 ARM*
	1 LEG
WRITE-OFF FOR BEING A GOOD PATIENT	*1 ARM*
NOW DUE	**1 LEG**

You may well find my sense of humor to be a bit bizarre. I'm okay with that. But know that the ability to laugh has carried me through some pretty tough stuff in my life.

Humor and laughter are gifts from God which enable us to take our heavy situations lightly. When we laugh, endorphins are released, and we make our own little natural high. It's a very good and wonderful thing.

Before the surgery, there was one additional tough task: my first visit with a prosthetist. I had no clue that this would be done beforehand. When I received the call to schedule my pre-op visit I was a little taken aback. I went with some trepidation *(who am I kidding?—it was a considerable amount)* about the whole process.

I was also quite anxious about the cost. There was no way (I was afraid) that I could afford one of the modern prosthetics. The best of them ran up to $50,000. My bank account wasn't anywhere near there.

While I sat in the room waiting to meet my prosthetist, I felt a tumble of emotions. Surrounded by pictures of amputees and their prosthetics, news articles, model body parts, and sample parts of prosthetics resulted in sensory overload. I was rapidly being immersed into a whole new world.

Ron Goldstein walked into the room with a confident swagger and a broad smile on his face. He was talkative and willing to answer every single question I had. And he told me things I didn't even think to ask. What was clear to me from the beginning was his passion for his work. This man genuinely cared for his patients and was VERY enthusiastic about his work. He toured me through the entire operation at Arizona Prosthetic and Orthotic Services.

Back in my room, it was time to begin the construction of my initial prosthesis. Ron would make a plaster cast of my leg in order to form a socket for my stump. This would be placed on me in the operating room and I would awaken in the PACU with an initial post-operative prosthesis (IPOP). When not wearing the IPOP, I would wear a stump-shrinker to help the stump reduce in size in advance of a permanent socket. So much vocabulary to learn! There was something comforting to me in knowing that Ron would be in the OR with me. I had just met him but I liked him. Turns out that he is the boss, the owner of APOS. From that first meeting he has been wonderfully kind and supportive of me.

Thursday, April 5, 2007, Mother and I once again did something we had done together so many times before. We woke up early and headed to the hospital at an ungodly early time. I was Dr. Beauchamp's first case that day. It was dark when we left home and still dark when we arrived at the Mayo Clinic Hospital. All of that is so much my same story, just a different day.

Here's what was different. I was calm, cool, and collected. There were no preoperative "yips." For me, surgery doesn't get easier each time; it has always gotten harder. This time, however it really did seem that I had an uncharacteristic ease in my heart.

Before leaving the house, I took my bright fuchsia pink sharpie and wrote on my right leg: "Well done good and faithful servant!" I thought it was a reasonable subtext for the "yes" they would later write on my right leg.

"Righty" had been what I called my leg. Mama taught me, early on, to talk to "righty" and tell him it's going to be okay. Don't ask me why my righty had a male gender—it's just the way it started. Righty had been the battleground for much of the war in my body.

So many surgeries, casts, and therapists pulling on it, and now all of that was coming to an end. He had held up so strong and for so long. He deserved a proper send-off.

We were seated in the preoperative waiting room. I took out my cell phone and took a picture of my right foot. Then came the gift of a moment of laughter between Mother and me.

Once they took me into the pre-op area, I remained calm and resolute about the events that were about to unfold. The miraculous nature of the day was beginning to be evident. Calm with few nerves was the beginning. Next, the nurse was able to start my IV on the first attempt! Praise the Lord! Generally I am a "tough stick" and end up with multiple punctures. Or worse, the dreaded words, "It's a small vein; let's hope it holds until the anesthesiologist gets you to sleep, then doctor can find a better one in the operating room." This would make me more anxious than ever.

I have in the past had an inordinate fear of being conscious during surgery. It's a horrible and helpless feeling that you are completely out of control. The surgical team wouldn't know that I was conscious because of the paralytic agent, and I wouldn't be able to speak. Gives me the creeps just to talk about it. But today, we had a good vein and the IV was running properly.

Nerve blocks were inserted in a special procedure room and would be used to manage pain. I was sure all this meant that everything was going to be fine.

Nursing staff brought Mother back to sit with me until they were ready to take me to the operating room. Almost immediately my pastor arrived. Pastor Tim had a calm demeanor and a bright smile. He asked the nurse if I could be given communion. She agreed. And so on that Maundy Thursday, when we remember Christ's institution of the Holy Meal, I had communion. And with that, and hugs and kisses to my mom, they wheeled me away to the operating room.

My final memories are of practicing something my friend Jeff suggested years earlier. When I had told him of my pre-op anxiety, he said I should close my eyes and see all the people who loved me standing all around me and further remember that I was safe in God's hands and in the prayers of the people who loved me. I closed my eyes and the vision of my loved ones brought me such amazing peace. I knew there was a crowd who would be waiting in the visitors' waiting room. And, that the Lord would be with me.

And with that, I was out…

Waking up in the post anesthesia care unit (PACU) is a weird experience. Your eyes are open and you think you can hear things going on around you. There's time spent drifting in and out. What really brings you into startling reality is pain. Over the years I have become expert at making sure my first words are "It hurts." In so doing I do my part to make sure that the pain medicine gets going as soon as possible.

Today in the PACU was different. As my mind started to become clear, I noticed instantly that although I was uncomfortable there was no major pain. Hard to imagine, but the nerve blocks and the morphine were doing well.

My first conscious memory was looking down and seeing my prosthetic foot sticking out of the sheet. I remember thinking, *Well I really did it. The leg is really gone*.

It was not a dream. Reality. There were no feelings or emotions in that moment. Perhaps it was the influence of the anesthesia.

My next clear moment was seeing my friend Deb (a Mayo surgeon) standing over me. She's on the phone with her dad (also my friend, Ken) telling him that I am indeed out of the operating room and doing well.

"She's even awake," she tells him. "Do you want to talk to her?" And before I knew it, I was on the phone with Ken. A brief hello and affirmation that I was feeling pretty good, all things considered. It was almost surreal.

Because there was a delay getting me into my room, Deb helped arrange for my friends and family to come back into the PACU in shifts to see me. With each person, I marveled that I was doing so well. The morphine pump was available to me, but I was not pushing it constantly. It is such a weird feeling, to actually feel pretty good that soon after surgery.

Later in the day I was rolled into my room, still feeling pretty good. My family was lined up against the wall.

"Hi everybody! I'm so glad to see you!" Clearly the happy juice (morphine) was working.

"Is she on drugs?" Chad (Callie's brother, my nephew) asked.

"Yes," my mother answered. "Don't be too surprised at anything she says," she added.

Good thing she warned him. The rest of the day and evening I drifted in and out, even when I appeared alert, the medications kept me pretty drowsy. Non-sequiturs were coming out constantly.

A word here about Chad. He was thirteen years old at the time. He had asked his mother for permission to miss school so that he could be at the hospital that day. He is a wonderful young man who has been my buddy since he was a baby. Chad has also traveled with me for speaking engagements. He and I share a love of sports. He is a kind and gentle soul. One of the things he does best is work with children in Vacation Bible School. Recently his summers have been spent as a Bible Camp counselor. I'm now running the risk of embarrassing him when I tell you that he is tall and good-looking. Oh well, part of the job of adults is to embarrass children.

So when Chad asked to be at the hospital, it said so much to me. He was there out of concern for me and for his grandmother and his mother. That is the kind of young man he is. Later in my hospital stay, it was to Chad that I first introduced "stumpy." He told me I was weird especially since I wasn't all that drugged up at the moment. We laughed. Lord—I do love that kid.

My first twenty-four hours post-op were relatively uneventful. Physical therapy began by getting me to stand on my leg and prosthesis. Therapists (occasionally known as "physical terrorists") are always more anxious to move and begin therapy than are patients.

Part of the challenge for me is that I have no upper-body strength to hold myself on crutches. I use them but literally hang from them. No real function on the left side from the nerve injury and subsequent bone loss coupled with a right wrist that doesn't bend and a right elbow that barely moves equals a real challenge for both the therapist and me.

The therapist used a walking contraption to stand me up, using my elbows to stabilize me. I use that word cautiously as I wasn't even close to stable. Oh, and then there is that gait belt, which they wrap around your waist. Who are they kidding? If I'm about to fall, they will never catch me by pulling back on that thing.

In that first day, Ron came to be part of my initial steps. He was there to make certain that my IPOP was functional. There are no words to adequately describe the flood of emotions I felt when, after standing, it was time to sit back down on the bed. Ron showed me the lever to pull to enable the mechanism to bend. When I did, I sat down by bending both knees for the first time in memory. I was a very young child the last time that happened. I sat down like a normal person. I did not do the old butt drop, I actually sat down. Yes, I felt "normal." How weird is it that I felt normal and I was an amputee. How wonderfully made by God are our psyches when we can feel normal and whole less than twenty-four hours after such traumatic surgery.

And as usual, when I am excited or delighted by something, I burst into tears. Crying is an expressive outlet for me. They were tears of joy. Poor Ron and the therapist, they had an emotionally overwrought woman on their hands. They handled it like professionals. I think I even saw a tear in Ron's eye.

My pain was reasonably well managed by the nerve blocks and medication. Push the button and a little morphine kicked me back into a sleepy disregard for the pain. I had the sensation that my foot was still there. It was weird but not uncomfortable. I had been warned about the concept of phantom pain but prayed that it would be something limited. So far, so good.

Friday started out about as well as can be expected. The second postoperative day can have you experiencing more pain. There are two primary reasons for this: first, they begin to back down the amount of pain medication, and second, physical therapy kicks into a higher gear.

Sleep is also a factor. I, like most people, don't sleep all that well in the hospital. And on the second day there is a physical (and consequently emotional) fatigue that begins to play a role. Fatigue diminishes the ability for the body to handle pain.

I was intellectually ready for the second day. But that intellectual readiness falls away when the difficulty to be faced comes into clarity. So it was for me. Friday started a bit tougher but I was able to make it through therapy sessions. The sensation in my now missing foot was major. And more than feeling like it was there, I felt the need to scratch an itch. This was not fun. Itching can be nearly maddening.

By evening the phantom sensation began to change from that annoying itch to full pain. It was hard for me. Perhaps it was even harder for my family. They had come from church after attending Good Friday worship and could do nothing to ease my discomfort. They were left only to hold me as I fought against it. It was only after I was given medication for pain and sleep that they were able to go home.

Night is often difficult for me when in the hospital. Usually this is because I can't sleep, feel uncomfortable, and/or there's nothing on the television worth watching. Hospitals rarely have cable TV.

This night was the worst in memory. The phantom sensation turned into phantom pain. Agonizing pain. I wrote in my diary: "it feels as though my body is remembering and reliving the pain of being cut apart… Actually it feels more like being ripped apart."

My foot (the missing one) felt like it was in a vise grip and being twisted and crushed simultaneously. It was unbearable. It is still almost unspeakable.

My nurse had come into the room to help me to the bedside commode. As she did, I cried out in pain. Attempting to comfort me she said, "It's okay to cry; I know it hurts."

"I cannot, I must not complain," I said.

"Yes, you can, you have every right," she gently said.

"No, no," I replied. "Not on this night, I must not complain on this night, not when my Savior is suffering horrible pain on the cross, pain he suffers for me."

I almost couldn't believe the words that came out of my mouth. Feeling an almost out-of-body experience, it seemed as though I was watching myself from a distance.

Certainly the words I spoke were true. I believe nothing can compare to the physical pain Jesus endured. And on Good Friday, I have always attempted to keep that physical suffering in my mind. It is an essential part of the Holy Week/passion experience. Easter has meaning when understood in the context of the events that precede it.

As much as I believe and openly share my faith with audiences large and small, a private moment like this one comes with more difficulty. I wish I was a stronger personal witness but it has not been my gift. Yet there I was telling a nurse I had known for just a few hours that I could not cry and complain on the day of Jesus's suffering. This was so not me. And yet I suppose it really was and is me.

The reaction of my nurse was beautiful. She helped me back into bed and told me that she was a Christian. She shared with me her faith in Jesus and that she, along with others working that shift, would pray for me. In her voice I heard the sound of peace and comfort that seemed otherwise so elusive. In that moment she was a healer.

Skeptics might say that prayer was not answered because the pain, the awful pain, did not relent. Through the night and into the next day it was so hard. And so exhausting! Pain wears you out. Fatigue and pain are a tough pair. But what the skeptics don't understand is that I survived the night because of those prayers. They reminded me of the beautiful fact that I was not alone.

Thankfully, there are breaks in the pain cycle. Sometimes the break can coincide with the peak of the pain medication. There is the thirty minutes when the meds are at their strongest and your body relaxes into a drowsy respite. Short-lived as it is, it is still a timeout from the pain game.

Relief can also come through distraction. Therapy does wonders in this regard. When your entire focus is on standing or walking, it shuts other things out. Don't get me wrong; there is some discomfort in the therapy sessions, but there isn't enough energy to move your body and fully recognize the pain. The only bad part about distraction is that when it is over, the pain comes rushing back. Pain has the temperament of a two-year-old. "Look at me, look at me," it yells, and it is always using its outdoor voice.

With all that and with my family and friends taking turns sitting with me, Saturday passed. When the pain came, it came big. My body would twist and jerk and writhe in an attempt to get away from it. As the day passed, I began to fear the night. Would this be another like last night? *Please, Lord no*, I prayed. Really, I begged.

Again, the night was dark and seemed so very long. This night may have been worse because I knew how bad it could get. I braced myself for the challenge, but to no avail. The horrible pain, the feeling of the bones being twisted and crushed, came back with a vengeance. Saturday night was a repeat of Friday. Yet there was a difference, and it wasn't a good one. A new fear began to compound the pain. Fear loves the darkness. This night brought the fear that this pain would be with me for a long time. Was this to be my lot in life? Was this what they meant about "persistent phantom pain"? I had read about it and knew that it occurred on rare occasions, but I began to fear that I would be one of those rare cases. It seemed an oh-so-dark future.

Fear multiplies pain and divides your strength for the battle. Positive self-talk and breathing techniques seem like muskets used against a foe armed with nuclear weapons. They are all you have but it's nearly impossible to defeat a persistent enemy.

It was a night spent clinging to the rails of the bed. Tears flowed until I had no more. My prayers were erratic pleadings with the God I knew was near yet seemed beyond my reach. It was dark and it was awful. I verged on a dark night of the soul.

At six a.m. I was at my emotional end and wanted my mother. Fifty-one years old and I'm not ashamed to tell you I needed my mother. She could at least hold me through the worst of it. I had held off until six a.m. because I thought she would be up and getting ready for Easter worship service. My family would be going to church together, and part of me didn't want to get in the way of their Easter celebration.

As a Christian, Easter is the great festival of our year.

We join together to proclaim the Risen Christ. Gratitude to God and joy in the promises of Jesus fill worship. It was hard enough to be in the hospital on Easter, but I shouldn't take that from my mother.

Shortly after six a.m., however, I gave in to my need for the comfort of my mother. I called the house and there was no answer. Had she left already? I tried her cell phone and again, no answer. Before I could get too worked up, I remembered their plan to attend Easter sunrise worship at six-thirty. Yes, she had left the house and there was limited cell phone coverage around the church.

Easter sunrise service is special at that parish. We can sit outside and watch the morning light break over the mountain. It is such a God-filled moment as darkness is once again vanquished by the light. Hope replaces the despair of Good Friday's crucifixion. Life is new all over again.

Reflecting in that moment about the sunrise worship brought sufficient calm to my mind and body that something remarkable and, to me, miraculous occurred. In direct proportion to the calming of my heart the pain began to ease. By six-thirty a.m., I was in a place where I could do what I desperately needed: sleep. Rest was, in that moment, the right prescription.

I awoke to one of the most beautiful sights I have ever seen. My family, dressed in their Easter finery, standing around me. Mother, Julie, Callie, and Chad seemed nearly aglow. Their smiles were Easter smiles. Happy is hardly sufficient to describe how I felt to have them there with me. Hopeful is a far better word. In their faces I saw love and, when the feeling of being loved is present, there is hope in all circumstances.

Turns out I am not a rare case. On Sunday morning the horrible pain seemed to break. There would be bolts of big pain, and that nasty itchy feeling, but I was fully ready to take them over the crushing pain of the previous two days and nights. I was doing well enough to actually take a walk outside of my room on the prosthesis with the aid of my extreme walker and therapist. Life outside of the hospital room is an important step toward recovery.

I was even allowed to have the IPOP off for a short while. This was important because it allowed me to touch, albeit through the bandages, my leg. Touch has always been a part of the way I cope with my pain. Mother had taught me this a long time ago along with this encouragement: "Talk to Righty, tell him it's going to be all right, tell him to settle down." Righty is now Stumpy, and I treated him with all the old tricks and they worked. My family had to take a breath and adjust to the name Stumpy, but I loved it instantly.

Easter Sunday brought me other visitors and time to be involved with people more than with pain. Sometimes (and I'm being honest here) visitors can be more draining than comforting. People who graciously take time to come to the hospital should be welcomed warmly. The problem comes when the visit lasts too long and/or visitors ask me to recount the events of the past few days. Sometimes I end up cheering up the people who have come to bring me cheer.

Easter was delightful. One of my visitors was my pastor and his wife Lorrie. They brought a lily from worship and a picture of the sanctuary adorned for worship. Best of all, when Lorrie came into the room, she hopped up on the bed and we talked, face to face. Now you may ask, what's so great about all that? Well, I can tell you. I have never been able to sit on the bed face to face with a girlfriend. My leg has always been something I had to work around. In that moment, however, it was wonderfully casual and spontaneous, two things that were nearly impossible for me to experience. Special seats at the theater, special shoes to support my deformed feet, cars, and planes all came with considerations. Lorrie, now sitting exactly where my leg would have been, made me happy. That day I was just a woman who had a visitor and where she sat was no big deal.

Interesting of course is the fact that casual spontaneity didn't remain beyond that point. If ever there was a circumstance in which planning is required, it is being an amputee. Gone are the days of jumping in the car and going somewhere without consideration for accessibility. Oh well!

The remainder of my hospital stay went as per plan. I was just at the beginning of being an amputee. Each day I walked a little farther and took a little less pain medication. Both were indicators that I was healing. I had anticipated a stint in a rehab facility, but the doctor felt that I would do better to go home, rest, and heal, before starting any rigorous rehabilitation program.

Repeating the ritual from so many other hospitalizations, my mother and Aunt Carol packed me up and brought me home. I was able to make transfers from wheelchair or electric scooter to the bed, and first the commode then the toilet and eventually to a shower bench. Days were challenging at first. Finding a routine and ways to do the activities of daily living were not easy but they did come. My mother had long ago instilled a "can-do" attitude so there was nothing else to do. I had to figure out ways to get things done. And I did.

Learning to walk on a prosthesis was another challenge. The IPOP was cumbersome and didn't feel at all like a leg. Soon Ron would have me into his office and begin construction of a new socketing system. After that I could wean myself from the crutches.

Those early days were a roller coaster ride. And I'm not talking about the fun kind. One day would be good and I would feel optimistic about the future. And the next might be 180 degrees the opposite. Inconsistency is challenging. Sometimes the prosthesis went on well and I had no real discomfort in wearing it. And then there were days when I worked for as much as an hour to get the pin lock mechanism properly engaged. The sheer mechanics of putting it on were difficult for my arthritic hands and less-than-fully-functional arms. It could be physically exhausting. On those occasions, the emotional toll was huge.

One day at a time became more like one hour at a time. The inability to look too far forward was depressing. Everyone likes to think of a brighter tomorrow. I, however, had to operate in the present moment. Anything else began to seem too big, scary, and intimidating. When you are barely coping in the moment, anything beyond that felt impossible.

There is also the very real issue of postoperative depression. It comes as a result of the bad cocktail that is anesthesia, plus pain, plus pain medication. I gotta tell you, that was hard. I'm an optimistic, future-oriented person, so looking ahead used to give me hope beyond my current circumstance. Now I felt no extra energy for the future. I was barely keeping above water on a day-to-day basis.

When I was ten weeks post-op, Mary Lee took off for a long-planned white-water trip on the Colorado River through the Grand Canyon. This was discussed before the surgery and my doctor was confident that I would be doing well by that point. However, I would need to have someone with me. Aunt Carol had my uncle to care for. My sister, a full-time job. So it was Carol's daughter, my cousin Amy, who we turned to for rescue. She was living in Texas and wasn't currently working. Willing and able to help, Amy flew into town a day ahead of Mother pulling out of town.

Amy and I were raised like sisters. As adults, we have taken different paths. She married shortly after high school and had four children. At the time, she had two grandchildren and shortly after would have two (now five) more. We have not spent the time together we would have liked. It happens that way, one day you realize ten, fifteen, twenty years have passed. Family gatherings were fewer and even geography hindered our ability to spend time together.

Love, real love, allows for the lack of time to just be a fact of life. It does nothing to alter a relationship based in real love. I love Amy for many reasons, not the least of which is her big old heart. A woman of tremendous compassion, she has the ability to take life in stride and never stop caring. She, like her father my Uncle Dallas, would do anything she could for anyone. Having no real idea what she was in for, she was willing to come and care for me. We had a great time together. Manicures and pedicures (my pedicures were now half-price) and new hairdos left us acting like teenagers again. Long talks and junk food equal good times.

In August we had our annual HAG vacation, this time to Reid's home in the mountains. I was delighted to be able to walk throughout the cabin and needed crutches only when we went out shopping. Bathing was tough, but I am a master of the sponge bath. (*Too much information? Perhaps.*)

Clearly I was making progress. But it was difficult. Every day presented a challenge of some sort or another. The stump was healing well but the socket was just plain uncomfortable. It was hot and, in Arizona, that's double trouble. But the real problem with the socket/prosthesis is the way it forced my body to twist and turn.

I have a typically rigid, arthritically altered body frame. The physics employed to make the prosthesis bend and straighten use muscles in the back and hip that were not being used in the same way when walking on my previously fused right leg. Once you begin to alter the rigid frame, there is a chain reaction of unintended consequences. More work for the remaining foot/ankle and knee causes pain and further joint damage and destruction. In order to do "this" you risk or, in fact, damage "that." I said then that I could handle the amputee thing, but in conjunction with the juvenile rheumatoid arthritis it became exponentially more difficult.

The recovery road was long and challenging. My grandmother had a saying she used about handling a difficult situation. She would say: "You can get 'it' done with the help of God and a good outfield."

By the grace of God, days passed and I grew stronger.

It seemed so slow, but when looking back I can say I did better faster than I thought. And I did have a great outfield. Ron became not just my prosthetist but also my friend. I saw him often, sometimes weekly. He was always available to me and worked hard to find ways to keep me comfortable and mobile. He was even kind and empathetic during my emotional lows. When I got frustrated and depressed, he kept refocusing me on the positive. His passion for helping people is inspiring.

I have a physical therapist who I am glad to also call my friend. Andy Clary was my PT long before the surgery. His ability to get movement out of my arthritic body is amazing. I am convinced that his efforts allowed me the balance needed to not only adapt to the prosthetic, but to also make transfers when the prosthetic is off. Andy was a very successful collegiate athletic trainer; his National Championship footballs are on display. When you are in his "gym," you experience his desire to get you back into the game.

So much to learn, and things that must be allowed for when planning even the shortest vacation. My life had changed as much, if not more, than my body. Would I ever get to a sense of ease? Would it ever get to be a casual reality rather than an issue impacting every aspect of my life? More questions than answers.

Nearly five years of working hard to work it out have passed. It has not been easy; nobody told me it would be.

One thing to which I cling is that I do not regret having the surgery. It helps knowing that once in the operating room, Dr. Beauchamp discovered that the entire fixator-mechanism in my leg was loose. Literally,

A FOOL AND HER LEG ARE SOON PARTED 253

it was sliding around within the bone. A fall or bump of any significance could have led to a bad break of the femur, which could have been life threatening. As loose as it was, it likely would not have held up to additional metal plates and screws.

Surgery was the right thing to do and knowing that has helped to keep regret from taking residence in my thoughts. There are no regrets for me. It has been hard—really hard. Regrets—none. Thanks be to God!

Making hard decisions is something few people want to do. Me included. And yet life, our all-too-human condition, can bring the need for a difficult choice to our front door. When the going gets tough, the tough go…shopping…?

Where do you go when the going gets tough? How do you make the hard choices in your life?

Do you find times of decision-making, particularly when the choices are less than ideal, opportunities to grow closer to God? I have never subscribed to the thought that God chooses things for us. It was not God's will for me to be sick. He wasn't trying to teach me anything when I had my amputation.

God's will is for us to live full and complete lives in celebration and gratitude for His grace and love in our lives. That very fact is so radical that it propels and compels us to reach out with that same love to the world around us.

Now who wouldn't want to take any and every opportunity to lean into that? Even if it means making tough decisions.

Good and gracious God,
Strong and Loving Lord,

I find comfort in the words of the Psalmist when it is written:
"Even though I walk through the darkest valley—
You are with me"
for it is Your strength alone which makes my life livable.
It is Your love alone which makes my life open to other joys
and it is Your grace which sustains me throughout
the toughest moments of this life and
grants me the peace to wait for the life
You promise into the future.

Amen

15

The Promise From My Father

The quality of mercy is not strain'd,
It droppeth as the gentle rain from heaven
Upon the place beneath: it is twice blest;
It blesseth him that gives and him that takes…

—*The Merchant of Venice* by William Shakespeare

As I shared earlier, my father was not ready to be a father when I arrived. He wasn't anti-children, he just wasn't "ready." I'm not sure whether he had more wild oats to sew or was just plain terrified of the responsibility. I'm guessing some of both would be closer to the truth.

My father would retell the story of me being thrust into his arms by the nurse. We come from a family of storytellers, and the good stories get retold over and over again. This was one of my favorites, probably because I thought it was about me. In reality it was all about my father. He described the panic in his heart when the nurse thrust me into his arms. He was such a great storyteller that the moment seemed almost comical. That's how he played it. We all would laugh. Tragic would be a better descriptor. As all tragedy contains comic elements, our laughter could have been tears. My dad was actually scared of parenthood and resentful of the situation. And I'm quite certain that he was neither the first nor the last father (or mother for that matter) to feel this way.

Society pressures parents into what is, for some, an artificial joy. Aren't you delighted and excited about this baby? Well, why not? So it was for my reluctant father. He knew his life had changed and would likely change even more in the coming days, weeks, months, years.

My father grew up in a less-than-ideal situation. He was one of six children (two older sisters and three brothers). He was born in 1925 and raised in Hemingway, South Carolina. Parents Napoleon Bogan Sturgeon and mother Atwell Zurilla Altman raised their children in poor circumstances. Daddy called their home a tarpaper shack. I never really believed him, until we visited Hemingway and I saw firsthand.

My grandfather, called Bogan by most, had difficulty supporting his family. The Great Depression not withstanding, times were hard in the swamp country of South Carolina. Bogan's life course was altered when Daddy's younger brother, Mallon (age four at the time), tragically fell into the vat of hot water used for washing clothes. Bogan heard his son's scream and ran to him only to pull the child's limp, lifeless body from the vat. Grief sent Bogan to a place from which his family said he never fully returned.

Atwell came to the marriage from a large family and worked in the tobacco fields. She continued to do so after marriage and children. Atwell's youngest sister (Bertha) tended to Atwell's kids (or young-uns) along with the other nieces and nephews. Atwell loved her Lord and raised her children faithfully at the First Baptist Church.

After Mallon's death, Bogan took to attending and even preaching at the tent revivals that were held out in the country. My father had to sneak away to see the revivals because his mother did not approve of all of that "hootin' and hollerin'." She did not even allow the children to see their father preach. She did not like the revivals and knew that Bogan was not of a clear mind.

Daddy quit school after the sixth grade. Not at all unusual for the times, it was sad because he had such a bright and intelligent mind. He worked in the fields and/or did whatever jobs he could to help bring money into the household. His mother, however, knew that Paul's life would hit a dead end if he stayed in their little town. She wanted more for him. Shortly before his fourteenth birthday, she gave him a small amount of cash she had saved and encouraged him to go make something of himself. He left home and got odd jobs, some in exchange for room and board. Reading books and watching movies brought him the education he missed from school. When he could, he sent money back and even occasionally visited his mother. He worshiped the ground she walked on.

Daddy went into the Army Air Corps and was in Europe during World War II; at the end of the war, his unit was among the last to return to the states. While waiting to return, Daddy got word from the Red Cross that his much beloved and sainted mother had died. Like most of the "greatest generation" he rarely spoke of that time other than to say that grief nearly did what the Germans couldn't: kill him.

Grandmother Atwell's death brought one of the greatest stories I've ever heard. Of course I never met her, but I did meet her sister Bertha. Bertha brought this story to life and I felt transported to that hospital room on that day as I sat and heard her speak.

Atwell had been bedridden from stomach cancer for some time. Bertha visited her twice a day. It was their practice for Bertha to read scripture during her visit. The Bible was opened and God's Word was read from whatever page was before her. They believed that God would lead them to the proper Word for that moment.

In her final days, Atwell had grown increasingly agitated. She repeatedly asked to be taken to lay in a "cool stream." "I know I will be fine if I can just find a cool stream," she would say. Bertha could always calm her as she so loved to hear the Word of God.

Bertha came into her room this day. Atwell was again asking for her "cool stream."

"Now, now," Bertha said, "let me tell you God's Word for today."

Although those words had always brought peace to Atwell, this day she remained decidedly agitated. She wanted her "cool stream." PERIOD.

But all Bertha could do was what she always did. She grasped Atwell's hand and opened the Word of God, just as they had done for their entire lives. She let the Bible open on its own, trusting that God's will would be revealed in this fashion.

The Bible opened to Revelation 22:1. Bertha said softly, "Atwell, hear this from God." Bertha began reading: *"Then the angel showed me the river of the water of life…"* Atwell grew still.

Bertha continued. *"It is clear as crystal, flowing from the throne of God…."* At once, Atwell sat up in bed and said, "Bertha, there's my stream and I'm going home." With that she lay back and died.

"Safe in the arms of Jesus." This is the inscription on little Mallon's headstone. And it was Grandmother Atwell's strong belief that dying was indeed "going home." Her trip home was likely down a cool stream that led her to the gates of heaven.

My father returned home from the war, still deeply grieving the loss of his mother. He also found that his father had lost all of the money that my father had sent home to be put in the bank. His father had fallen victim to scam artists and con men. He gave money to every charity he heard on the radio. And the money he gave belonged to my father. The relationship between my father and his father was never fully repaired.

I actually know more of my paternal grandfather from my mother than from anything my father ever shared. There was so much brokenness there that I think it pained my dad to speak of it.

I spoke once by phone with my granddaddy. He was in failing health and my parents made plans to travel from our home in Tucson, Arizona, to South Carolina to see him. There was no grand reconciliation between my father and his father. Perhaps there was just too much between them, or perhaps it had something to do with being men of that age.

Sharing this helps me to explain the way in which my father was parented, which explains in part the way in which he parented. There was no role model or mentor in whose steps he could follow.

The one thing my father did was show deference to and support for the decisions of my mother. We never heard "wait until your father gets home." She ran the children and we knew he supported her completely.

With regard to my health, my father played a different role. He was loving and supportive. But the medical stuff made him queasy. Mother handled that part with ease.

So he did what he could do. He put his wonderful voice and powerful salesmanship to work as a fundraiser for the Arthritis Foundation. Paul could have sold icemakers in the frozen tundra. Getting people informed and then enlisting their support was a natural fit. I even joined him for some of his speeches, making a great teaching tool. The cute kid on the crutches could coax donations out of the most hard-hearted. I loved the time spent with him like that. The spotlight and the applause were great for both of us. We were a wonderful team!

This book is not the place to retrace the entire family history. Suffice it to say that, as with most people, the older I got the more I saw the flaws in my parents and their relationship with one another. The hurt between them grew, and the strain on my mother pained me greatly.

I was in high school when they divorced. In that time my father was quite a disappointment to me. He acted in what I deemed to be a selfish manner. There were very hard times, particularly in the beginning. Times when I didn't want him around. Tincture of time is often the best prescription. So it was, as I aged I moved from a childlike disappointment in a fallen hero to a peace with an imperfect man.

Martin Luther wrote that we are all "fully saint and fully sinner." My father was all of that—loving, passionate, and flawed. I came to understand that grace is the free action of God to love us unconditionally. Understanding grace allowed me to choose to love my father for what he was, rather than resent him for what he was not. Choosing forgiveness released me from being hostage to my childhood expectations. Forgiving him did not mean that I approved of his behavior. The power of forgiveness lies in its ability to release us from bondage to brokenness and pain. Forgiveness is the road into the future charted by embracing, rather than approving, the past.

As an adult I came to love my father. And my father came to love being a father. He was known to say that he had found the joy of fatherhood twenty years late. His recognition of the missed years seemed more than penance.

It was my sister Julie's twenty-first birthday dinner. Daddy had taken us out to the Chaparral Room at the wonderful Camelback Inn. Fine dining was something we all enjoyed. Yet he was not feeling well that night, and even complained that he had been experiencing "mild nausea" for some time. He could be a bit of a baby about his health, so we were not alarmed. We simply encouraged him to see a doctor. "Call Mama, and she'll get somebody to see you." That ended the conversation.

A few days later, I knew he had an appointment with one of the faculty doctors at Mother's office. Truthfully, I expected it would be just the ticket to settle his mind. Nothing would be wrong. So, my heart sank when I saw Mama and Daddy arrive at our house that day after work. They were friends at this point in their lives. He was at our house frequently. But this seemed different. It was. We gathered in the living room, making that sort of end-of-the-day small talk which comes readily when nervous. We all were on edge.

Finally, he spoke. "Well, kids I gotta tell you, your papa is sick." With a matter-of-fact tone he told us that there was a mass in his liver. Doctors suspected cancer and would be certain upon return of the lab results. Mama filled in the medical gaps for us.

"Now I want you to know this," he said. "I don't want to die, and I'm going to fight this however I can." He continued, "But if I do die now, I will be okay and so will you."

There were hugs and tears and the resolute Sturgeon spirit emerged. We take our medical lumps of coal and charge forward.

In the weeks to come, he underwent liver resection surgery. My six-foot-four 230-pound father seemed to shrink before my eyes. The recovery was hard and yet my "big baby" Papa took it like a soldier. From early November to spring the following year, he went through really tough times. He became a regular at our house, especially for Sunday dinner, because my mother could get him to eat. And he grew stronger. His liver was regenerating. We were all so hopeful.

In May, Julie graduated in the Centennial class from Arizona State University. Daddy was excited to see his daughter graduate. He was feeling good and looking good. Almost like before. It was a great day of celebration for our entire family.

Less than a week later, tests showed that the tumor was growing back. Two weeks after that, his bile duct was blocked and he was hospitalized. His poor liver function led to hallucinations, and his skin itched as though he'd been stung hundreds of times. High-dose narcotics were used to help him be comfortable.

Hope dwindles quickly when the reality of cancer's lethal power is recognized. There was nothing more that could be done, so Daddy set about making ready for the end. He created a sort of bucket list of people he wanted to see. There were meals he wanted to have, and time he wanted to spend with the people he loved.

The summer of 1995 was crazy hectic. People came and usually stayed in our home as he had only a small apartment. My sister moved back home after a very brief attempt at a summer job in Montana. She would have more summers; he would not.

In August, Mother and Julie took a long-planned white-water raft trip in Idaho. Daddy insisted that they go and promised not to die while they were gone.

Promises were important to my father. If you make a promise, it must be kept. We refer to this as a "daddy promise." He would make seeming commitments that would "fall through" (his words) but a promise was different. Promises are an unbreakable bond. He was alive when they returned. Barely. Although still in his apartment, the morphine was causing him to have violent hallucinations. I was scared for him, but knew I couldn't physically move him to our home without my mother.

The day after their return, Mama and I went to his apartment. She told him it was time to leave his house. As she helped him to the car, he stopped and said, "Promise me you are not taking me to the hospital." There was that word: "Promise."

My dear mother calmly replied, "No, Paul, you are coming home with me. No hospital, I promise." He rightly trusted her and came without complaint.

He remained in our home until his death. Friends from the hospital brought a bed and supplies, and we converted a bedroom into a hospital room. Doctors made certain that Mother had the medications necessary to keep him comfortable. Her training as a nurse was invaluable. Mother, Julie, and I were his caregivers.

In the first couple of days, he rallied. His medications were managed and he was eating better. He was cogent and conversing freely. Those days are treasures to me. We took the opportunity to talk on a real and intense level. Past hurts and wrongs were just that: past. No need to revisit them. Being in the moment brought tremendous clarity to our relationship. He was my father and I loved him, foibles and all.

And he loved me. He knew me and my weaknesses. He loved me with them, not despite them. The time we missed mattered so much less than the moments we had at hand. I celebrate that gift of time with my father. And in that time he gave me one final gift, a promise.

"Don't be so sad." This was his way of encouraging me. He told me I would survive this and that he would be okay. "Besides," he said, "you are so much like me that I will always be a part of you. Just like your papa, you will get better, stronger, and more beautiful with age. The best is yet to come—I promise."

Again, that word: promise. I knew he meant it, and that "daddy promises" always come true.

Two days later, he slipped into hepatic coma; three days afterward, he passed away. We had prayed for him to peacefully return home to his mother. We spoke those

THE PROMISE FROM MY FATHER 265

permission-giving words to him, and we promised to love and remember him well. It was a daddy promise.

The past can hold many of us back from the present and future, especially in our relationships. May I suggest a reading of the parable of the prodigal son from the Gospel of Luke. This is a story that appears to be about two very different children. Although there is plenty about these two from which we may learn, the parable is about the father. And, all parts serve to enlighten us as to the true nature of God, the Father.

Is there a past hurt or hurts that continue to pain and wound you? Consider looking at them as part of your story. And when you place them in the context of your story remember this: YOUR story is not finished. How will you write your next chapter?

Remember, love and forgiveness dwell in the heart and home of the Lord. Love and forgiveness will lead you home. Jesus promised!

*Good and gracious God,
Heavenly Father,
We sing from the hymn "Amazing Grace,"
"Your Grace will lead me home."
Let those words sink deep into our hearts
so that in all circumstances we may be reminded
that You stand, arms open wide,
to celebrate homecoming with us.
Allow us, Father, to find peace in our hearts and lives
and to give peace to those around us.
We are counting on Your promises, Abba Father.*

Amen

16

When Losing the Battle Means Winning the War

I have fought the good fight,
I have finished the race,
I have kept the faith.

—2 Timothy 4:7

Here's the problem with a book that takes almost four years to write. The story changes and lives evolve over time. It was my intention to write my life's story up to the point at which I became an amputee. My reasoning was both selfish and simple. I believe this is common when one reasons with themselves. Our "self" has an uncanny instinct for self-preservation. Perhaps that is part of God's grand plan. I shall, one day, inquire. Simple reasoning is rarely either. The amputation would be the end of that part of the story. I had to stop somewhere, and that seemed an obviously simple place to me.

Perhaps there was even a hope that this (the amputation) would be a launching pad for a bold new era in my life. I'd have two functional knees. Gone would be the days of stressing over seats on airplanes and in movie theaters. My Pollyanna rose-colored glasses were clearly on. And inasmuch as the old limits would be gone, why not stop the book at the operating room doors?

The selfish part comes with a confession: I was hoping to perhaps one day write a second book. It would be a book on the new life I was leading in follow-up to my first book. I thought this second book would continue my message of hope. Okay, I also hoped it would be a best seller. I would get booked on *Oprah* or *Ellen* and from that there's always a possibility of a movie deal. I could then afford the beachfront home in Maui where I would sit on the lanai and live the life of a famous speaker and author.

OMG! I am not just selfish; I am delusional.

I have now lived life as an amputee for almost five years. In that time I have become keenly aware of the reality of my "new life." It has caused me to re-examine many of my life choices and pray for new vision and guidance from God.

I have shared that the first year was a time of frequent adjustment, discomfort, and uncertainty. This is very much the standard course for people following surgical amputation. Time is needed for the body to heal. Fitting and adjusting the prosthetic system is ongoing as the swelling in the remaining limb goes down. With each adjustment of the mechanism, there is a sort of concomitant mental adjustment needed. The entire process brings such a rise and fall of emotions. Every day is different and with that comes uncertainty.

My first year brought with it the realization that

my pre-existing rheumatoid arthritis would be a greater complicating factor than anticipated. As much as I like to say "I can do it," there are indeed times when I can't. A positive, hopeful attitude is essential, but it cannot mitigate the enormity of the challenge presented by my body.

Ron (my prosthetist) was always willing to try something new to make the prosthesis work. From making orthotics for my left shoe to changing the length and angles of the prosthesis, we tried it all. He did all this to make the prosthesis work comfortably.

I learned to walk on the prosthesis and did so with great pride and joy. The feeling of triumph and accomplishment was great. A real rush for me, it was also something for which I received praise and affirmation. I am like a puppy in this regard: if you praise me, I will do whatever I can for more praise.

By Christmas (eight months post-op) I was feeling better, thanks in large part to the cooler weather. I could walk so long as it wasn't far. Distance was the enemy; as stamina waned, fatigue set in, the kind of fatigue that would literally stop me in my tracks. I always looked for chairs and benches when I was in public because in those moments when fatigue took over, I could not move another inch.

And another word came powerfully into my daily vocabulary: SWEAT. Not the kind of perspiration from being overheated, rather the kind that comes with no exertion and feels like your body has turned into a Rain Bird sprinkler. I sweat so much that it was poured out of the socket at day's end. And I ruined clothing, all the while using heavy-duty antiperspirants.

Not all of my clothing was ruined by sweat stains. The prosthesis was a hard surface upon which I sat. Even though Ron padded the socket, it was still hard on my clothing. Skirts and trousers got caught and became "holy." I had a brand-new pant set to wear to a friend's wedding in Mexico. I sat on a concrete bench and stood up only to find holes in my pants from the two hard surfaces rubbing together. I have always taken pride in my appearance and found the wardrobe challenges of being an amputee particularly stressful. Everything had to be so much larger to fit over the prosthesis. (I suppose I have complained long enough.)

In February, not quite one year after the surgery, I was invited by the Grand Canyon Synod's Planning Team to their Lutheran Seniors Assembly, also known as the Rally in the Valley. They invited me to be a keynote speaker at the gathering of the "Senior Saints," which annually attracts between 300 and 400 people. The theme of the 2008 Rally in the Valley was "It Is Well With My Soul" and focused on wellness and wholeness.

I had a little chuckle about a gathering with the theme of wellness and wholeness inviting a person with a chronic disease and a less-than-whole body. Later I actually used that line in my speech. Afterwards the event organizers told me it was precisely for that attitude they invited me.

My message focused on the persistent grace of God, which carries us forward when we cannot move ourselves. It was exactly what I needed to hear for myself. Through the trials and tribulations of the past year, I was still standing, still walking, still believing that I was going to be a successful amputee.

My speech was well received as indicated by the standing ovation and many kind comments following. I was delighted to be back making a speech and sharing the story of God's love in my life. The fatigue in my body was overwhelmed by the joy of proclaiming God's grace. It was so affirming and reinvigorated me for the ministry.

From that sense of triumph, I garnered great strength to face year two. Ron had come to see my presentation. Afterwards, he shared with me his idea to reconfigure my socket to a brimless variety. This meant the socket wouldn't be as high on my leg and perhaps less uncomfortable for my back, and maybe even easier on my wardrobe. I was thrilled!

The brimless prosthesis was a wonderful thing because it was indeed more comfortable. Less torque on my back was a welcome relief. Shorter socket did mean some "relearning curve." Basically the longer brimmed socket was easier to control and engage, while the shorter version required more of my own muscles to be at work. All in all, however, I was excited about the newfound comfort in this brimless iteration.

With my newfound comfort, I began walking more and more. And with more walking came weight loss. Losing weight has always been a challenge to me, so this weight loss was a delightful side benefit. And the more I walked, the more I wanted to walk. Fatigue remained an issue, but in the first few months of the new socket it seemed less problematic.

With weight loss also comes the need to refit the socket. This is done initially by adding socks and padding. More layers equals a hotter and less comfortable wear. Add to that the 100-plus degree summers in Arizona, and I began to walk less. This meant that I had to deal with my weight being a "moving target." And shifting weight leads to shifting socket fit. In turn this leads to discomfort, sometimes even major discomfort.

Fall's cooler weather meant I could get back to walking; some days even walking with ease. I was feeling well enough to travel to North Dakota for a Junior High Youth Gathering. I was so intrigued when the group invited me because their scripture was from Romans 10:15: *How beautiful are the feet of those who bring good news.* It seemed a perfect fit for me. My attitude was strong and confident.

The trip was wonderful. It's hard to imagine saying a trip to Minnesota/North Dakota in mid-November is wonderful, but the opportunity to work with the great folks of the Northwest Minnesota Synod is always such a treat! Sharing time with young people who are seriously examining their faith is a blessing. Plus, Chad went along for the heavy lifting, selling our "Gimpy by Grace" first edition T-shirts, and having some good old fun with Aunt Paula.

We worked hard for three days. By trip's end, I was exhausted and desperately needed to be home. Fatigue was so significant that it is only by God's grace that I got home. The good news is that mother was at home and ready to nurse me back to health. This had been the plan. She did exactly what she always did, and I bounced back.

A month later, I was doing relatively well. Still with ups and downs, but overall I was pleased. Perhaps 2009 was to be the year in which it would all come together. This was my prayer.

Let me back up a moment. Toward the end of 2008, I began to have difficulty with the skin on ol' Stumpy. I could walk, but the skin was beginning to break down. When this happened, I had to rest the skin by staying out of the prosthesis, meaning walking on crutches and one foot. Hard? Yes, it was! But I did it. When necessary,

I did have my electric scooter for around the house. We did not own a car rigged to carry the scooter. Thankfully, the grocery store and big-box discounters offer electric carts. I was getting by, at least that was the story I was telling myself.

My old friend Jeff made a trip to Arizona that fall. I wanted so badly to show off how well I was doing, as this was the first time since just before the amputation that we had been together. Truthfully, that was how I often felt about it. "Show off how well I am doing" is a sentence I have spoken or thought with some regularity. It is that optimistic, can-do attitude that has been my trademark. People are inspired by it and I am praised for it. I am after all, the "happy cripple."

This has been my modus operandi for so long that I can't really point to when it began. Perhaps it was in my childhood. Being a genial child was impressive to adults. I loved being told that I was such a nice, brave girl. Pat the puppy!

I also learned early on that nobody wants to be around a complainer. My family generally knew the true situation, but I guarded my pain from the rest of the world. I had a tough enough time making social connections and therefore tried to keep my health in the background.

My standard response to "How are you?" was, "Well, thank you." You may call that guarding or self-preservation. And that may well be a part of the answer. I believe it is also a product of my upbringing, which focused on manners.

The rest of the answer likely has more to do with denial and a feeling of being resolved to my reality. Denying the pain somehow took away its power to control my life. If acknowledged, the pain could alter my life course and potentially lead to an inwardly focused spiral downward. My entire life has been about being resolved to the reality of being an arthritic. Now I was getting that same resolute focus about being an amputee.

Just keep going, that's what I always do. Pain medication, rest, whatever it took, I did it. Giving up or giving in was never an option.

During one of my follow-up appointments with my orthopedic surgeon, Dr. Beauchamp, I told him about the pain I had been experiencing in my left foot, ankle, and knee. I was not looking for a surgical answer but rather wanted him to know that my body seemed to be having a difficult time adjusting to the prosthesis. You must remember that I trust this man implicitly. Yet when his next step was recommending that I see a rheumatologist I was forced into an uncomfortable place. I had a long-held disdain for rheumatologists.

Now, I'm not here to criticize this specialty. My feelings come from long-ago experiences. Back in the day, when the field was beginning to expand, all too often people were offered false hope and little choice. Had I been diagnosed with rheumatoid arthritis in my early twenties, there is a reasonably good chance that I would not have had the surgical intervention I did. In those days, medicine was the prevailing game plan. I could not help but wonder about the quality of life I would have had without my early surgeries.

The argument between surgeons and rheumatologists has merit on both sides. Rather than spend any additional ink taking one side or the other, let me leave it at this: I have been loath to consult a rheumatologist. Yet here I was with a body that was growing weaker. As 2009 began, I was back to a constant pain. Not always from the effects of the prosthesis, more often my arthritic body was the source of the problem. With a hard swallow of my preconceived notions, I reluctantly agreed to see a rheumatologist.

By this time I was spending more time in a wheelchair than on the prosthesis. Constant left foot pain made walking more than a few steps out of the question. The pain was such that I hurt whether weight-bearing or not, although weight-bearing was thought to be a contributing factor. Dr. Beauchamp had ordered x-rays and an MRI to determine the nature of the problem in my foot/ankle. No easy answer was to come. What I had was a foot/ankle **full** of arthritis. No easy answer for that problem.

And then there was my left knee. It too had been radiologically examined. Significant arthritis was noted and the need for joint replacement was discussed. Dr. Beauchamp had said I would know when the time would be right. My left knee had held up like a soldier, and I was not yet ready to surrender my own joint for a mechanical implant and the long-term maintenance, which would ensue.

Neck and shoulder pain I experienced were due to walking on crutches. Beyond the actual pain, it caused me difficulty sleeping. Without sleep, the cycle of pain becomes difficult to break. And then there is the ever-present challenge of my rigid frame and constant back pain.

This is the body that I took in to see Dr. April Chang-Miller. I brought with me my lengthy health history and my all-too-thinly veiled skepticism of rheumatology. After a nearly two-hour interview and thorough physical examination, Dr. Chang-Miller had gathered the preliminary information she needed. She ordered additional laboratory tests and a bone density study. Once the results were available, I was to return and a treatment course would be designed.

Our first meeting went well and I left with some respect for at least **this** rheumatologist. Perhaps I had misjudged. That's always a risk when judging.

When we returned to see Dr. Chang-Miller, she continued to win me over. Mother goes with me on visits such as these because we are a team. We need to hear the information together so that we may jointly face the days ahead.

Dr. Chang-Miller said I had pretty good lab results and my bone density was great. Imagine that! Her recommendation was some vitamin D and a basic nonsteroidal anti-inflammatory drug (NSAID). She acknowledged what I knew. Most of my pain is from long-ago damage done to my joints rather than from a more active arthritic flare. Disease-remitting agents were not in the plan at this point.

"Bright lady," I thought. She was giving it to me straight and without sugarcoating. By far, I want my physicians to be straightforward and honest. It is not their place to shield me from the truth. Perhaps I had found a rheumatologist I liked.

Then she lowered the boom. The "bright lady" had my number. "You," she said "are an active person, correct?"

"Yes, I truly want to be an active person," I replied.

"Do you know when to stop?" she asked.

"I stop because I have to."

"Well, are you really taking care of yourself?" There was the boom!

Without repeating the back and forth, suffice it to say that Dr. Chang-Miller gently yet firmly led me to understand my own accountability for my health. She encouraged me to get more rest and to not over-stress my body. Choices must be made to allow for my body to do the things I really wanted. Gone were the days when this body could take whatever damage I inflicted upon it and bounce back. Her closing comments were to encourage me to spend some time reevaluating my life. "Make some choices and take care of yourself" was the best advice she gave me that day.

Stiff upper lip, can-do attitude, buck-up, and get on with it had always been the ways I dealt with life's challenges. Pain would be a factor and therefore I just didn't think there was any other way. Dr. Chang-Miller had stirred up so many thoughts in my mind, and the feelings were most unsettling. Not only did she bring home the reality of my very damaged body, she led me to challenge all my preconceived notions about the way to lead a productive and happy life.

There was to be no immediate epiphany. In fact, my meeting with the doctor stirred up a hornet's nest of feelings and made for a most difficult time. It is hard enough to contend with my painful and limited body, but this stuff went straight to the heart of my self-identity. Who am I if not the person who keeps on keepin' on? After all, I believed it was my persistent courage for which I received praise and affirmation. This puppy wasn't ready to give up on getting the pats I so loved.

Prayer was my refuge. When thinking things through

brought only more confusion and more unanswered questions, prayer was a place of calm. I have always prayed in a simple conversational style and so, when talking to myself was way too uncomfortable I talked to the Lord. Although I have never heard the voice of God speaking, I have experienced those moments in prayer when great calm comes over me. I believe that calm is a way in which the Holy Spirit is affirming what I'm saying and/or doing. God's Holy Spirit works within us, guiding us toward His perfect will.

I may have been in the midst of an outward identity struggle but felt that my inward identity as a child of God was settled. How then could I find balance? How do I bring forth that inward self to let the other take a nap?

Years earlier I had made a commitment to myself, more accurately a written contract, to operate from a keen awareness that I was indeed a strong and lovable woman. (Claiming that identity occurred just before my return to the faithful community known as church.) In so doing, I acknowledged myself for who I knew, deep down inside, I already was. Strong and lovable were the words I chose because they felt like the two things that, if I remained clear about them, would shape and inform my life.

When I returned to faith, my contract seemed all the more appropriate. I was strong and lovable because that's the way God created me. Two of my favorite pieces of scripture speak precisely to this point:

> John 3:16: *For God so loved the world that he gave his one and only Son, that whoever believes in him shall not perish but have eternal life. For God did*

> *not send his Son into the world to condemn the world,*
> *but to save the world through him.*

> Psalm 121: *I lift up my eyes to the mountains—*
> *where does my help come from?*
> *My help comes from the LORD,*
> *the Maker of heaven and earth.*
> *He will not let your foot slip—*
> *he who watches over you will not slumber;*
> *indeed, he who watches over Israel*
> *will neither slumber nor sleep.*
> *The LORD watches over you—*
> *the LORD is your shade at your right hand;*
> *the sun will not harm you by day,*
> *nor the moon by night.*
> *The LORD will keep you from all harm—*
> *he will watch over your life;*
> *the LORD will watch over your coming and going*
> *both now and forevermore.*

As the days passed, my heart was in the early stages of change, moving in a new direction. After days of attempting to resolve my work/life/body issues, my focus shifted toward real identity. I am **not** my work. My value is as a child of God, not as a "happy cripple." A "happy cripple" may surface occasionally, and when it does it must be real and genuine. It should not be a mask I wear, nor an act I perform.

I have lived a happy, productive life knowing of God's love, and yet it was a remarkable thing to regain that focus. My preaching and speaking had always been truthful from-the-heart proclamations. Now I was hearing my own message. Once we know better, we are empowered to do better. And by doing better, I mean making new choices, charting new paths, and making the kind of life changes that allow us to operate most fully from our identity as a child of God.

My choices would be made in alignment with my identity. This was the first step and formed the framework for all future steps and choices. First, it was important to define my "rule out" options. These would be things, away from which I was unwilling to turn. Chief among those would be quitting the work to which I truly felt called. Preaching and teaching are my God-given gifts and so I chose to retain the opportunities to do so.

Church work tends to run in cycles. I'm busy for a few weeks and then there are stretches of time when I am not. This is a challenge but one I choose to retain and address as needed. I made the commitment to myself to say no when it was important for me to rest. Giving oneself the permission to say no, even to a good thing, is wonderful.

So my work in the church would remain. What else could I do to smooth out my hectic life? This was a perplexing question. Ultimately, so much of my life revolves around the church that finding other things to "cut" seemed futile.

Back to prayer. Truthfully, prayer for me is an ongoing conversation. Perhaps, therefore, it is better said that my prayer life shifted a bit. I needed the Lord's guiding, as I felt faced with very few choices. That's hardly even true; I couldn't see any choice at all.

Prayers tumbled around my consciousness asking for the leading of the Spirit. Where else could I make changes to my life in order to preserve my health? This would be a much more difficult question to answer. My prayerful struggle would take time and eventually come to a most astonishing conclusion.

One particularly difficult day, my pain level sent me to bed. It was on that day that the answer began to present itself to me. Honestly, I was just plain tired, more exhausted from the pain. Perhaps because of the pain, or maybe fatigue from the battle, I was headed toward a classical episode of "Gimpy gets gloomy."

Depression often dances into the party on the heels of pain and/or fatigue. On this occasion I was really challenged by the pain. My father's word for it would have been weary, and weary aptly describes that time. Weary of the pain, weary of the exhaustion, you name it—I was weary of it all.

In my prayers I told the Lord that I didn't want to hurt anymore. I was tired of being brave and just wanted it to stop. This was a new prayer for me. Strength and courage were always what I prayed for, so why for something different did I pray this day? That prayer wasn't even very realistic. I had a damaged body from a chronic disease. The pain wasn't going to go away. I knew that, so why was I bothering the Lord with this request?

It became a sort of tennis tournament in my mind. "Won't go away" versus "Please make it end." From it all, I was mentally as well as physically weary.

The following morning I was awake but not rested. I took my electric scooter to the kitchen for the morning ritual of coffee with my mother. While sharing with her my long night, I told her that I was tired of fighting the pain. Somewhere in our conversation I rolled the scooter toward my crutches to take them up in preparation for beginning the day.

"Why don't you just use the scooter," Mother said. "There's nothing to be gained by putting yourself through the ordeal of crutches." That was brilliant, but then you knew that about my mother, didn't you?

THERE IS NOTHING TO BE GAINED FROM PUTTING YOURSELF THROUGH THE ORDEAL.

That statement opened the door to a new choice. The scooter was a real option, rather than the crutches, for tough days at home. In choosing the scooter, I could save my arms, especially the pits and maybe my left foot/ankle/knee. It would not necessarily make the pain stop, but I could keep from inflicting further damage. Although I wasn't ready to give up on the prosthesis, using the scooter more liberally was a positive move.

When I discussed this plan with the doctors, they were pleased if not fully on board. Although no physician readily counsels patients who can walk to turn to a scooter or wheelchair, mine were pleased that I was finding ways to save myself. A trial run would show if this was worth pursuing.

The electric scooter wasn't the best solution. Our home is generally accessible, but the scooter was larger than some of our doorways and thus a challenge to maneuver into and out of rooms, most notably the bathroom. Plus, the scooter was an older model that could not hold a consistent speed and could/would lurch forward and/or stop suddenly.

Despite my best efforts to limit the wear and tear on my joints, I continued to experience pain. And more than pain there was more/continuing destruction of my knee and foot/ankle. After trying a brace for my foot (which was beyond ugly) and a new pair of specialty shoes, there was still no relief for my foot/ankle.

Dr. Beauchamp had me evaluated by a Mayo Clinic foot specialist. The bottom line was hard to hear. Surgical reconstruction of the fusion of my left foot/ankle was the only surgical option. The difficulty with the procedure was the requirement for me to be non-weight-bearing for a minimum of eight weeks. People with only one leg don't do non-weight-bearing very well. It would necessitate wearing the prosthesis all the time, even at night, in order to get up to the bathroom. No thank you, I will pass.

By the early summer of 2009, the reality of a wheelchair (power chair) was becoming quite clear. My arthritic body was in full revolt, and the pain of wearing the prosthesis limited my lifestyle. I was becoming nearly homebound. For the first time in my life, fear of pain began to enter my decision-making. Helpless and hopeless were increasingly accurate descriptors of my mindset. I also wanted to do whatever it took to keep from requiring additional surgery. If using a power wheelchair meant that I could anticipate a brighter future and a return to activity with fewer painful side effects, then that is what I would do.

It's just not that easy. Despite some advertising, which may appear to the contrary, buying a power chair is not a snap. Medicare has a slew of regulations that govern the approval of said devices. Beyond the mountain of paperwork, there is the cost. Power chairs do not come cheaply. Add to that the fact that a power chair, which cannot be transported, has minimal value. Our vehicle would not hold the lift mechanism for the chair, and so a new car had to be in the equation somewhere.

Then there was also the problem of my pride. I found it tough to deal with the power chair. But harder still was the minivan that would be ideal for the lift mechanism. Recall earlier I said I needed to make choices that support better health and consequently allow me to live into my identity as a strong, lovable child of God. Pride could completely derail that intention. So it was time to kiss my pride *adios!*

Here was the key to accepting this new phase in my life. I made a very clear choice, as revealed in prayer, to surrender. I have been a proponent of surrendering to that which cannot be changed for a long time. This time I was choosing to surrender to that which felt better. It meant leaving behind my personal whipping stick that I had used to force myself to push through the pain and discomfort in order to keep going.

Upon public surrender to a power chair, a burden lifted from my shoulders. People reacted a bit like they did when I announced my amputation with a standard kind of "oh no." This, however, was different in that their concern was for my feelings. Most knew of my strength and inner drive for mobility and independence, and ergo were concerned that I had been forced into a wheelchair and that I was saddened by it all.

With a smile on my face I reported that this was a good thing. And I was genuinely excited. Perhaps I couldn't make it stop hurting, but I could quit hurting myself. There was no value any longer in putting myself through the ordeal.

> "Amazing grace—how sweet the sound—that
> saved a wretch like me."
> Sweet Grace

Having conquered my emotional reluctance to accept a power chair, I now had to face the reality of the financial challenge. Time and patience were necessary to get the paperwork approved through Medicare, but there still remained my share of the cost of the chair and lift mechanism, plus the purchase of a new vehicle, which were not in the financial plans. Because I went on disability at such an early age, I have very little retirement savings. On my disability income, we give to our church and pay the bills. Our car was paid for and running quite well. I needed a power chair and did not have the thousands of dollars necessary to pay for the non-covered portion of the power chair or the lift, let alone the car.

To a few of my friends, I shared my angst and my dilemma. I did so because that's what we do; we share our burdens with our friends just as we share our joys. Living in a Christian community, we are blessed to have around us the people who want to be present without regard for joy or sorrow. All experiences are worth sharing and in so doing connect us one to another. And more importantly, connect us all the stronger to Jesus. In Jesus, we find the duality of life and death, joy and sorrow, existing together and keeping us in the faith.

My friends rallied around me. Marcia and Nancy (can-do women of the first order) took up the cause of creating an event with the intent of raising funds for my power chair. Parishes where I have worshiped and served joined the cause. Desserts and beautiful music (thanks, Karen) on the patio at Living Water Lutheran Church was the setting for a gathering of friends. Friends who wanted to help me. The event was called "Sweet Grace."

I was nervous about that night. I love to be center stage, but this was uncomfortable for me. The love people were expressing in words and in the sharing of their wealth was overwhelming. Gracious love poured over me with such tenderness that I felt a wholeness I had not felt for a long time. Love has a way of doing that, filling in our cracked places and allowing us to know our true worth. That night I felt as though I had a glimpse of what a bride feels on her wedding: beautiful, glowing with the knowledge of being loved.

Another amazing thing happened that night. I received a tremendous affirmation of my ministry. Words of thanks and encouragement for the work to which God has called me were shared freely. People wanted me to have my power chair so that I could continue speaking and preaching God's Word.

As the evening drew to a close, I felt so fully loved! I expressed my extreme gratitude to event organizers and participants. Because of their generosity, I was able to commit to them that: "The proclamation of God's grace would roll on!"

The choice between hotdogs and hamburgers notwithstanding, most choices require us to give thought to and weigh options before making them. Choices can be tough! If they were all easy, I suppose life would be boring. I for one would not mind a little boredom occasionally.

Do you have a standard way in which you make decisions? Are you a jump first, think later person? Or are you so methodical and analytical that you struggle to make even a minor choice? Most of us will likely fall somewhere in the middle.

Choices and decisions can get pretty sticky. This was what I faced with the power chair and, before that, the amputation. Not all of our decisions have easy options. Some, in fact, force us to make choices between what my grandmother called "the lesser of two evils." These times call upon our most important resources, not solely for the "deciding" but for the "living with" part of the choice as well.

When the time comes to make a choice, in which direction do you turn? Do you gladly accept the challenge that making a new choice may bring, or do you resent the need to change anything at all? Are changes something to be embraced or avoided?

We learn from Jesus and from the apostle Paul of the dynamic nature of our Christian lives. Nothing this side of heaven is guaranteed with the sole exception of the abiding grace and love of our Lord. And that is sufficient!

Indeed, grace rolls on …

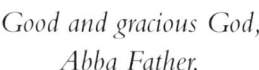

*Good and gracious God,
Abba Father,*

*You are the Potter and we are the clay,
the work of Your hands.
In praise and thanksgiving for Your gracious love
and abiding presence in our lives,
we pray for Your Holy Spirit to guide and direct us
as we navigate and travel this journey of faith.
Allow us to seek Your wisdom and truth
as we make choices and decisions in our life.
Let our lives glorify You.*

Amen

Postscript

"Love is forever."

—Mary Sturgeon

By invitation, I have shared my story with many and various groups across the country. My speeches are well received and I have been blessed by many kind words of affirmation. At these events, people often ask me if I have written a book or have a video, which they may purchase. My answer to this "squirmy situation" has always been a gracious non-answer. "How kind of you to ask; perhaps in the future."

LIAR—LIAR—PANTS ON FIRE!

I resisted the idea of writing a book for years. That's not entirely accurate—I fought it. Refusing to consider the notion that anyone would be interested in reading about me seemed humble, appropriately humble, perhaps even virtuous. Even as I write this, those thoughts seem absolutely ridiculous.

The call to write this book came from my maternal grandmother, Mary Sturgeon. When she first expressed her desire for me to write a book, I was taken by surprise. I knew she was proud of me and the woman I had become. Yet this was a much greater expression of affirmation than I had any reason to expect. This was a rather grand gesture from someone who just did not make grand gestures. More to the point, rather than a gesture, it was far more a heartfelt expression of her love for me.

Clarity began to come to me as I prepared to speak at her funeral. My grandmother was a great storyteller and I wanted to honor her by telling her story. She was not the storybook, hearts and flowers, cookies and cake, sweet-as-pie sort of grandmother; she was part cheerleader and part guilt-based drill sergeant. Born in 1905, the third of eight children and the first of only three to graduate from high school, she lived through the roughest times of the last century, including two world wars and the Great Depression.

She married the love of her life (my grandfather, Clifford) and had three children. The oldest, my mother Mary Lee, was followed by a son, James, and then another daughter, Carol. Theirs was a simple life with Grandfather working for the phone company, and together with Grandmother raising a family and tending a small farm. It was always described to me as an idyllic place to grow up, even though it had no indoor toilets. What they did have were gardens, orchards, chickens, pigs, a cantankerous horse, a pony for the kids, and Bossie the cow. Working on a farm, even a small one, is hard work. Hard work can, however, be beautiful, particularly when faced with love. Such was the case for my grandparents and their children.

No one could have foreseen that Bossie getting pregnant would lead to a series of events that brought this beautiful situation to a tragic end. As Bossie's milk dried up, my grandparents had to find a new source for the family's milk. They began buying from a neighbor, a common thing for those days.

Within two weeks grandfather became ill with what was thought to be the flu. His symptoms worsened and he was eventually diagnosed with typhoid fever. Mother and Carol got sick as well. The Missouri State Department of Health became involved because of the rarity of typhoid fever in mid-winter. They tracked the source of the disease to the milk the family purchased from their neighbor. Once tested, it was determined that the neighbor lady (and friend) was a typhoid carrier. Her lack of proper personal hygiene led directly to the tainted milk.

My grandfather succumbed to typhoid fever in March of 1941. Mother and Aunt Carol eventually recovered, leaving my grandmother a heartbroken single mother with three small children. She relocated the family to Kansas City, Kansas. There she had the opportunity to find employment and be close to her family. She could be mom, but her children, especially her son Jim, needed the father-surrogacy of uncles, scoutmasters, and churchmen.

Storytelling was grandmother's great gift and one of her supreme talents *(Her fried chicken, mashed potatoes, and gravy probably top my list)*. Her mind was sharp (even to the end) and her ability to recall details and place them in either a poignant or a playful context was brilliant. I remember hearing the story of my grandfather's illness and death and being struck by how real the love they shared was and remained. My grandmother and grandfather were in love; always had been, always would be, even to the end. Their time together on earth was, tragically, too short. She told that, as he neared the end, he said to her, "Mary, I have finally found what I have been looking for all of my life." To which grandmother replied, "What?" "God," he said. Taken aback, Grandmother said, "Oh, Cliff, you are a good man, you have always known God." But he insisted, saying, "This is different, Mary, God is the birds and the trees and the flowers; God is love."

God is love! This is the lesson Grandmother taught by the way in which she lived her life. She expressed her love by telling stories. In all honesty, I did not recognize this for a very long time. Regrettably, it wasn't until after her death that I awakened to the beautiful and loving intention behind her encouragement for me to write my story.

My grandmother had been present throughout my life. She had a front row seat to it all, watching me face childhood in the midst of adult circumstances. When my mother returned to the workforce, Grandmother was the first to hear of my trials and tribulations at school. Although my age and circumstance changed, she was for me a constant. She had seen this story as it unfolded.

Grandmother believed I had a story to tell. She believed in me, often when I did not believe in myself. So, I confess that, God forgive me, before her death, I committed to her that I would indeed write my book. She was dying and it seemed to make her happy. The problem was it nearly scared me right into the grave with her!

I truthfully had very little intention of writing a book. It seemed that, the longer I waited, the more stressful the task became. Things changed, however, when my life took yet another major turn with the amputation of my leg. There had been turns in the past, but this seemed different. Less like a turn, more like a twist. It was time to share this journey and share the story of God's abiding love. Through it all, grace rolls on.

You now know the full story of the previous turns in life's journey and may understand how this particular twist has changed my life. And changed it for the better.

My dear Grandmother,

I suppose it is inappropriate for me to say that a book is finished simply because my writing feels complete. I have come to understand that editing is a process that goes on and on until the book is actually printed. I have learned more than I ever thought I could about the world of publishing. All that said, I have left this for the last of my writing. I did so in order to stop, look back, and give credit for the impetus behind this book. Credit, dear Grandmother, is owed to you.

    For so many years you encouraged me, even badgered me, about writing this book. There were times I resented your persistence. From your front-row seat to so much of this book, you never wavered in believing that mine was a story worth telling. You believed in me when often I didn't believe in myself. And even though I didn't argue the point, you somehow

knew that one day I would face up to the challenge.

    This has been a really hard thing to do. I have visited painful memories and cried tears anew. My path has not been an easy one. There have also been wonderful experiences and loving people in this journey. Writing has given me the opportunity to feel huge amounts of gratitude, a blessing in and of itself.

    So now let me say that thing which is so often difficult for a child or woman to say to an elder authority: you were right! This is a good story, and it is worth sharing.

    I am grateful to God for the light you brought and still bring to me. One day I shall tell you so—face to face. Until then, you are always in my heart.

    Love,

Paula

About the Author

Paula Sturgeon is a self-described evangelist and itinerant storyteller. Whether it is a Sunday sermon or a keynote address to a national convention, Paula brings passion and humor together in a powerful and dynamic manner. Her message of hope centered in the love and grace of God has been well received by audiences. It is those audiences that have been urging her to write this book.

Paula Sturgeon was born in Kansas in the 1950s, and walked and talked at a very early age. This "picture-perfect" beginning was derailed when, at the age of fourteen months, she was diagnosed with polio. Two months later an additional diagnosis of juvenile rheumatoid arthritis meant that life would never be picture perfect. Since then, Paula has had more than thirty major surgeries, including an above-knee amputation. Each surgery was a step of faith, taken to make and keep her functional and independent. Paula now uses both a prosthetic limb and a wheelchair to remain active.

Paula shares a home with her beloved mother, Mary Lee Sturgeon. They continue to enjoy the journey as their partnership now includes the bridge table. Paula maintains a blog on her website www.gimpybygrace .com, and travels nationally when invited to share her message. Please contact her through the website.

*and it is no longer I who live,
but it is Christ who lives in me.
And the life I now live in the flesh
I live by faith in the Son of God,
who loved me and gave himself for me.*

—Galatians 2:20

Portions of the proceeds from my book are dedicated to these two charities. I invite you to join me in supporting them.

www.lunchesforlearning.org

Lunches for Learning Inc. exists to help break the cycle of poverty by providing nutrition and nutritional supplements to the very poor children in public schools, particularly in remote areas in the Republic of Honduras. This amazing organization brings together two important efforts. Children attend school (often in makeshift structures) and are fed a nutritional meal. It is a nonprofit organization that works through the cooperative efforts of individual contributors, corporate sponsorship, and the government of Honduras.

Although I am physically unable to be a missionary to a far away land, I am able to help make sure someone else can. Even the smallest gift works a mighty wonder. Consider this fact from their website: $15 will feed one child lunch each school day for a month and $150 will feed one child lunch each school day for a year.

www.callutheran.edu

I have been a longtime supporter of California Lutheran University. It is a wonderful academic institution and is committed to the concept of vocation. Recently they have begun development of a major in Theology and Christian Leadership designed to train students in specific areas of lay ministry and including four areas of specialization: Christian Education, Church Administration, Church Music, and Youth and Family Ministry. The curriculum will include religion courses as well as courses from other departments in the College of Arts and Sciences and the schools of Education and Business.

I had plans for a formal theological education that were derailed (as you have read) years ago. Now, I have a core belief in and commitment to the development of new leaders for the church. California Lutheran University is well positioned for this effort. I love God's church and pray these leaders through the power of the Holy Spirit will serve it.